Study Guide
to accompany

second edition
ENVIRONMENT

Raven • Berg • Johnson

Charlene Waggoner
Bowling Green State University

Saunders College Publishing

Harcourt Brace College Publishers

Fort Worth Philadelphia San Diego New York Orlando Austin
San Antonio Toronto Montreal London Sydney Tokyo

Printed in the United States of America

Wagonner: Study Guide to accompany *Environment, 2e*. Raven.

ISBN 0-03-025178-8

891 202 765432

USING THIS STUDY GUIDE:

Each chapter has a set of sections. Each section is designed to help you with the material in the chapter.

If you want to make the most of your study time while using this book, you will need to have additional paper for making cards and writing out answers. If you learn by listening, then get out a tape recorder and record your answers and information.

One of the best ways to study is to work with someone else. It is very easy to skip over material on your own. If you are working with someone else, you have to vocalize all of the answers. You learn by communicating. Also, odds are that if you do not understand something, a member of your study group will be able to explain it to you. Writing out your answers is a useful exercise.

LEARNING THE LANGUAGE:

One important aspect of studying science is language. Scientists from all over the world must be able to communicate effectively with one another. They create and use very specific terms to enable them to express ideas quickly. You already know many scientific terms. For example, you know what your stomach is and what it does. Stomach is a scientific word. You also already know what a 2 liter bottle is. Liter is a scientific term for measuring the volume of a liquid. It did not take you nights of studying to learn those scientific words. You work with them, you use them, you learn them.

The language of science is the easiest part of science to study and it is often confused with science itself. Unfortunately, knowing a scientific term does not mean that you know anything else about it. Knowing that the person sitting next to you is named Bob is useful and necessary information. However, the name Bob does not tell you anything about Bob. How old is he? Where does he live? How does he get to class? You need to learn more about Bob than his name if you truly wish to understand him. The same is true in science. You need to know the language so that you can communicate, but you need to think about the concepts in order to understand them.

Learning the Language is a list of the key terms used in the chapter. You could create this list on your own by simply highlighting new terms and ideas as you come across them in your reading. However, many students gain a sense of security from seeing a list of terms so it is included here. Use this list to learn the language and to begin to practice using the new words you encounter.

I

The easiest way to start is to make yourself a set of flash cards. Write the term on one side of the card. Write the definition and give an example on the reverse side of the card. Include diagrams and graphs to aid in the visual recognition of the terms. Silly mnemonic devices can also help with term recognition. Make up rhymes or acronyms.

Spend some time making your cards. The very act of thinking about what goes on the card as well as the physical process of writing it all down will help you learn.

Use the cards to study the terms. Look at the term and state the definition. Look at the definition and come up with the term. One of the biggest mistakes students make when working with flash card is that they stop repeating the definition. They look at the term and they say "I know that" and go on to the next. When they get to the exam, they find that they have learned the definition of the term as "I know that."

Simply recognizing each of these terms and being able to spell them properly is not adequate. To truly understand these concepts, you need to practice using them. Create your own critical thinking questions. Take the time to speak or write your answers clearly. If you occasionally make up a silly question, take the time to explain why it is silly.

CHECKING WHAT YOU KNOW:

Once you have had a chance to work with the language in the chapter, it is time to see what you know. Use the questions in this section to test your knowledge. You will also find this section useful for practicing your test taking skills. There are a variety of question types in this section. Many of the them ask you to directly recall the language you have been learning. Some of them will go beyond what is specifically covered in the text. In all cases, pay attention to how you are solving the problem. Practice your approach to each type of question. It will reduce any test-taking anxiety you may have.

Hints For Taking Multiple Choice Exams.

- See if your instructor has specified "choose the BEST answer". This means that there is one answer that is better than the rest. It does not necessarily mean that the rest of the answers are all wrong. Some of them may be true, but they do not answer the question that is being asked.

- If the question contains a lot of information, re-write the question in your own words. Some questions may take an entire paragraph and tell a story when they are really just asking for a simple recall term. For example, a question might tell the entire tale of little red riding hood and then ask who red riding hood was visiting. All the details about the goodies in the basket and the wolf are part of the story, but they are not essential to answering the question. You could rephrase the question and get to the proper answer.

- As soon as you decide an answer is not the best choice cross it off. This keeps it from coming back to haunt you later as you review your answers.

- If the choices are a list of terms, write a short one or two word definition next to each one. This will help you rule out unrelated terms.

- Do not get drawn into the "all of the above" trap. While in many cases that answer is present because it is correct, it is not always true. If you find one choice that is not correct, then "all of the above" is not correct. If you find two choices that are correct, then "all of the above" is probably the right answer even if you are unsure about the other choices.

Hints For Fill in The Blanks.

- These questions are typically asking for direct recall. This is where learning the language is useful.

- Look for clues in the format of the question. Perhaps the question blank is preceded by "an" instead of "a(n)". This may tell you that the answer is a word that starts with a vowel. Likewise, tense and plurals can also serve as clues.

Hints For True/False.

- Carefully read each statement.

- Look for the little words. Often it is the NOT or SOME or ALL that determines whether or not the statement is true or false.

◆ When practicing the true and false questions in this book, take the time to write out a statement explaining why the statement is true or how it is false. This will help you focus your thinking.

The next several sections are designed to get you thinking about the material you are studying. Not every chapter has every type of question. You will want to spend some time with each answer. You may have to refer to other chapters in the book to fully answer the question. Remember, what you are doing is thinking about the concepts.

Hints For Essay Questions.

- Make a simple outline of the key points. If the question asks you to discuss 3 things, be sure that you have all three things in your outline.

- Write in complete sentences. Unless the question specifically says "list three things," you need to write well. You do not want to lose points because your sentence structure is confusing.

  Example:

  "Global warming builds up of carbon dioxide in the atmosphere of burning fossil fuels and flatulence from cows"
  What does this mean?

  Global warming is caused by a build up of carbon dioxide in the atmosphere. The carbon dioxide comes from burning fossil fuels and flatulence from cows.
  Now it makes sense.

- Write legibly. You want to be graded on your ideas not marked down because your instructor could not figure out what "gznfic" meant.

◆ Do not add extra information just because you know something. It may detract from your point. It can make your instructor think that you are trying to hide a lack of understanding

IV

PEOPLE WHO MATTER:

There are some people who have made a major contribution to the field. Not every chapter contains this section, but it is useful to learn about the people who do the research. Often, it is useful to look at the times in which they did their work. It is instructive to see how far we have come or how far we have to go.

MAKING CONNECTIONS:

The questions in this section are designed to send you back to concepts that you have learned earlier and to preview upcoming ideas. You really cannot learn about environmental science in isolated chunks. Just as the organisms in the environment co-exist and are interdependent, so are the ideas and concepts you are learning. Spend some time thinking about these connections. Soon you will find that you are making connections on your own as you read through the text and read about the environment in the newspaper.

MAKING DECISIONS:

Use the information in this section to think about the issues discussed in the chapter. What you will need to be able to do to make a reasonable decision is:

- Separate the facts from the fiction.
- Identify any bias in the source of the information.
- Decide who is a credible source.
- Describe possible actions that can be taken.
- List the known consequences of each course of action.
- Make the best decision for you based on the facts and your own personal moral, ethical, religious, political, and social beliefs.

Carefully read chapter 2 in your textbook to get you started on the path to decision making. You will find that the hints are not complete in this section of the study guide. This is because you must ultimately make up your mind about each of these issues.

DOING SCIENCE:

This section gives you an opportunity to understand the scientific process. You will be asked to think about the experiments that were done to provide the information in the text. You will also be asked to design your own experiments to answer questions that are still unresolved.

The things you need to be able to identify when evaluating scientific evidence and designing an experiment include:

What is the **Hypothesis** that is being tested?
What are the **Controls**?
What are the **Results** of the experiment?
What interpretation has the scientist made from the results?
Are there other likely interpretations?
What are the assumptions being made by the scientist?
Are the assumptions hidden or acknowledged?
Do the data support the hypothesis?
Do the data disprove the hypothesis?
Is there a better hypothesis?

Table of Contents

CHAPTER 1 -- OUR CHANGING ENVIRONMENT

LEARNING THE LANGUAGE:

antagonism
atmosphere
biological diversity
cancer
climate
climate change
commercial extinction
community
consumption
deforestation
ecology
economic extinction
ecosystem
Endangered Species Act
endocrine disrupter
environmental science
environmental sustainability
exotic species
forest edge
fragmentation of forests
radiation

global climate change
green architecture
habitat
hormones
hypothesis
mortality
native species
natural resources
neotropical birds
nest parasitism
nonrenewable resources
overpopulation
ozone
ozone depletion
parasitism
parts per million
pollution
population
renewable resources
ultraviolet

CHECKING WHAT YOU KNOW?

MULTIPLE CHOICE:

1. Which statement is most accurate when describing the effects of human population on the environment?

   A. More humans using more resources cause less damage.
   B. More humans using less resources cause less damage.
   C. Fewer humans using more resources cause less damage.
   D. More humans using fewer resources can cause as much damage as fewer humans using more resources.

2. Along with population size, we must also consider _____ when studying the effects of a population on the environment.

   A. consumption
   B. conservation
   C. pollution
   D. population variation

3. _____ is the study of how humans interact with other species and the physical components of their environment.

   A. Environmental science
   B. Ecology
   C. Economics
   D. Resource management

4. The world's population is expected to pass _____ by the year 1999.

   A. 100 million
   B. 1 billion
   C. 6 billion
   D. 6 trillion

5. The intentional or unintentional introduction of exotic or foreign species into an ecosystem can cause

   A. native species to become threatened.
   B. native species to become endangered.
   C. disruption of the entire ecosystem.
   D. all of these answers are possible.

6. The zebra mussels in the Great Lakes are an example of a(n)_____ species.

   A. endangered
   B. exotic
   C. native
   D. indigenous

7. Which of the following is NOT a human-produced chemical that threatens the environment?

   A. endocrine disrupters
   B. CO_2

C. chlorofluorocarbons

D. water

8. A house built using post-consumer products, energy efficient technology, and recycled materials is an example of

A. passive solar heating.

B. sustainable marketing.

C. green architecture.

D. building a junkyard.

9. The gray wolf that has been reintroduced into Yellowstone National Park is an example of a(n) _____ species.

A. foreign

B. nonindigenous

C. exotic

D. native

10. Human _____ is causing great amounts of environmental stress and pollution.

A. conservation

B. consumption

C. creativity

11. Which of the following ecosystems is MOST sensitive to disruption and degradation by human activities?

A. Deep sea in the Atlantic Ocean.

B. Deciduous forest in Ohio.

C. Desert in Kuwait.

D. Grassland in Nebraska.

12. A(n) _____, if it becomes established, can threaten the ecology of its new environment and can contribute to the extinction of native species.

A. endocrine disrupter

B. chlorofluorocarbon

C. endangered species

D. exotic species

13. Overfishing in the Georges Banks is an example of

A. commercial extinction.

B. water pollution.

C. problems associated with global warming.

D. exotic species introductions.

14. How do endocrine disrupters work?

   A. They disrupt the circadian rhythms that all organisms use to maintain bodily functions.

   B. They alter reproductive development in males and females.

   C. They cause frogs to grow chicken wings.

   D. They displace species normally found in an area with species that are better able to compete for resources.

15. Environmental sustainability is

   A. the ability of the environment to support an unlimited number of humans.

   B. the ability of the environment to function indefinitely without going into a decline.

   C. the ability of the environment to recover from trauma introduced by humans.

   D. the ability of the environment to tolerate toxic chemicals.

16. Which of the following disciplines is NOT considered during the study of environmental science?

   A. Biology.

   B. Geology.

   C. Law.

   D. Economics.

   E. All of these must be considered in the study of environmental science.

17. Which of the following is NOT an example of how humans are making it more difficult for other species to survive?

   A. Spilling oil onto the land and into the water.

   B. Increasing in population.

   C. Introducing exotic species around the globe.

   D. Re-introducing species such as wolves into their native habitats.

   E. Consuming energy and raw materials.

18. In the diagrams below, each box represents the same land area and each circle represents a tree in the forest. Cowbirds are nest parasites. They lay their eggs in the nests of other birds, tricking the songbirds into raising the cowbirds' offspring. Which forest will have the highest probability of nest parasitism?

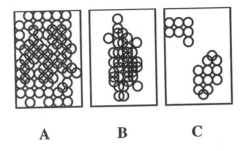

| A | B | C |

19. A controversial Danish study has determined that sperm counts in men have been declining over the last 50 years. This could be a problem because

A. men judge themselves by their sperm counts.
B. this correlates with an increase in the incidence of male reproductive birth defects and testicular cancer.
C. this correlates with a decline in the human population over the same period.
D. lower sperm counts are associated with oil spills.

20. Which of the following is NOT a factor affecting the environment that increases in severity as the size of the population increases?

A. People eat food.
B. People drink water.
C. People use energy.
D. People generate waste.
E. All of these factors affect the environment more as the population grows.

21. Construction firms across the country are increasingly converting trash such as used tires, aluminum cans, plastic milk jugs, and old copper pipes into

A. building materials.
B. trash burners.
C. wildlife refuges.
D. desertification projects.

22. In the future, we must be able to feed a world population almost twice as large as the present one without destroying the _____ that support us.

   A. nonrenewable resources
   B. governmental agencies
   C. biological communities
   D. green architectures

FILL IN:

1. The interdisciplinary study of how humanity affects other organisms and the nonliving physical environment is called _____.

2. _____ is the actual number of organisms present in a defined geographical area.

3. _____ are chemical messengers that regulate growth, reproduction, and other activities.

4. Many economically important fishes have reached _____ _____ because their numbers are so low that they are unprofitable to harvest.

5. _____ which is caused by urban growth, farming, and logging, has increased the probability that the nests of neotropical birds will be located at the forest edge, thereby making them more vulnerable to predation.

6. The combined effects of two or more pollutants may be less severe than the sum of their individual effects, a phenomenon known as _____ .

7. As the world's population has grown to ten times its former size, the level of carbon dioxide (CO_2) in the _____ has increased dramatically

8. The science of _____ is a discipline of biology that studies the interrelationships between organisms and their environment.

9. People consume a lot of _____ and water, use a great deal of energy and raw materials, and produce much waste.

10. Every human lives within a complex _____ of organisms, and our acts do have consequences for those organisms.

11. Broadly speaking, _____ _____ is the ability of the environment to function indefinitely without going into a decline from the stresses imposed by human society on natural systems (such as soil, water, air, and biological diversity) that maintain life.

12. Increasing population is placing a non-sustainable stress on the environment. As humans consume ever-increasing quantities of food and water, use more and more energy and raw materials, they produce enormous amounts of waste and _____.

13. The gray wolf, a(n) _____ _____, has been reintroduced in Yellowstone Park and the central Idaho wilderness because humans killed all of them earlier in the century.

14. Efficient use of materials and _____ in home construction is just one way that people have responded in recent years to pressing environmental concerns.

15. Stratospheric ozone absorbs harmful _____ _____ from sunlight.

16. During the Earth Summit, many delegates spoke about the need to deal with _____, the degradation of once-fertile arid and semiarid land into nonproductive desert.

17. The ability of the environment to function indefinitely without going into a decline is called _____ _____.

18. Ozone thinning was first hypothesized by two chemists at the University of California based on calculations they made in 1974 of the atmospheric effects of _____ (CFCs).

19. Our "progress" in developing _____ _____ has led to other challenges: the Georges Bank has been fished to commercial extinction, and neotropical bird populations are declining, in part because their breeding habitat-- the forested areas in North America-- is increasingly fragmented by development.

20. _____ _____ is interdisciplinary because it uses and combines information from many disciplines: biology (particularly ecology), geography, chemistry, geology, physics, economics, sociology (particularly demographics), natural resources management, law, and politics.

21. The dumping of chemicals used in industrial processes is an example of _____.

22. The invasion of zebra mussels in the Great Lakes is a problem because such _____ _____ upset the balance of the species naturally found in the area.

23. Environmental scientists are growing increasingly concerned that the rising levels of atmospheric CO_2 may change Earth's _____ .

24. Two or more pollutants interacting in such a way that their combined effects are more severe than the sum of their individual effects is a phenomenon known as _____ .

25. _____ is the study of population dynamics.

26. Increasing energy efficiency, conserving wood, and recycling discarded materials are all features incorporated into _____ _____ .

27. Haddock and similar economically important fishes have reached _____ _____ in the Georges Bank because their numbers are so low that they are unprofitable to harvest.

28. We are using _____ _____ such as fossil fuels as if they are present in unlimited supplies.

29. _____ _____ , such as cerulean warblers and olive-sided flycatchers, are faced with changing environments in both their winter and summer homes, and loss of habitat appears to be the main reason for their decline.

30. One important conclusion that we can make about climate change is that the effects of human activities locally and regionally can have global repercussions, even changing the composition of the _____ .

TRUE OR FALSE:

1. True   False   People in developed nations consume a lot of food and water, and generate a great deal of waste.

2. True   False   Fewer people using more resources cause the same amount of environmental damage as more people using fewer resources.

3. True   False   Human acts do not have consequences for the organisms around them.

4. True   False   Environmental science is the study of how organisms interact with their environment.

5. True   False   Environmental issues are often complex and complicated by different opinions about what should be done.

6. True   False   The Earth can support exactly 15.3 billion people.

7. True False   Success in achieving sustainability in population size and consumption can be accomplished by well-intentioned individuals in the United States alone.

8. True False   In 1950, only eight cities in the world had populations larger than 5 million.

MAKING CONNECTIONS:

What is the difference between a natural and an artificial chemical?

MAKING DECISIONS:

The U.N. conference on Environment and Development had a vast agenda. It was attended by representatives from around the world. Both industrial nations such as the United States, and developing nations such as Bolivia were present. Make two lists of concerns, from the perspective of a developed nation and of a developing nation. How would your perspective on biological diversity or sustainable development be affected by the conditions within each country?

DOING SCIENCE?

This chapter discusses chemicals called endocrine disrupters. These molecules mimic female hormones and are thought to be the cause of feminization of the males of some species.

You have found a pond downstream from a paper processing plant. This plant uses a lot of chemicals including dioxin. A unique species of frog lives in and around this pond. You have noticed that the reproductive organs in the male frogs in this pond tend to have more abnormalities and tend to be smaller than in similar species of frogs in other ponds.

Design an experiment, or a series of experiments to determine whether the differences between the male frogs of this species and other species are normal, or whether the abnormalities are caused by the proximity of the pond to the paper processing plant.

CHECKING WHAT YOU KNOW: (HINT)

MULTIPLE CHOICE: (HINT)

1. D
2. A
3. A
4. C
5. D
6. B
7. D
8. C
9. D
10. B
11. C
12. D
13. A
14. B
15. B
16. E
17. D
18. C
19. B
20. E
21. A
22. C

FILL IN: (HINT)

1. Environmental Science.
2. Population size or population
3. Hormones
4. economic extinction
5. Forest fragmentation
6. antagonism
7. atmosphere
8. ecology
9. food
10. community
11. environmental sustainability
12. pollution
13. endangered species
14. energy
15. ultraviolet radiation

16. *desertification*
17. *environmental sustainability*
18. *chlorofluorocarbons*
19. *natural resources*
20. *Environmental science*
21. *pollution*
22. *exotic species*
23. *climate*
24. *synergism*
25. *Demographics*
26. *green architecture*
27. *commercial extinction*
28. *nonrenewable resources*
29. *Neotropical birds*
30. *atmosphere*

TRUE OR FALSE: (HINT)

1. *True*
2. *True*
3. *False*
4. *False*
5. *True*
6. *True*
7. *False*
8. *True*

MAKING CONNECTIONS: (HINT)

Chemically, there are no differences between natural and artificial chemicals. Functionally, artificial chemicals are made by humans. Artificial chemicals often persist in the environment and have a greater potential for environmental harm.

MAKING DECISIONS: (HINT)

United States	Bolivia
food is plentiful	*food is less plentiful*
clean water is available for all reasonable needs	*clean water is not available for many people*
consumption life-style	*subsistence lifestyle*
By buying Rainforest Crunch, I can help preserve biodiversity	*Preserving biodiversity means that I cannot make a living off of the land. I will have to find another means to feed myself*

	and my family.

DOING SCIENCE. (HINTS).

1. Determine whether or not dioxin or another endocrine disrupting chemical is actually present in the pond.

2. Raise some frogs of this species from the pond in the laboratory in the absence of any endocrine disrupters. Do the males in subsequent generations have the same "abnormalities"?

3. Raise some frogs of a related species in the laboratory using water from the pond. Do the males in subsequent generations develop abnormalities?

4. Why wouldn't it be a good idea to transfer males from a related frog species to this pond? (Think about introduced species.)

CHAPTER 2 -- SOLVING ENVIRONMENTAL PROBLEMS

LEARNING THE LANGUAGE:

antagonism
cancer
carcinogen
climate
community
control
cost-benefit analysis
cyanobacteria
data/datum
death rate
deductive reasoning
disease
ecological risk assessment
environmental impact statement
eutrophication
experiment
experimental controls

global commons
hypothesis
inductive reasoning
National Environmental Policy Act
overgrazing
political action
prediction
principle
public education
risk
risk analysis
risk assessment
risk management
scientific method
theory
toxicology
variable

CHECKING WHAT YOU KNOW:

MULTIPLE CHOICE:

1. The cafeteria is serving mystery meat again. You have a bet with your roommate that there is no meat in mystery meat. In order to win the bet, you must convince your roommate. What is the best plan of action you can take?

   A. Use superior force on your roommate
   B. Test the mystery meat for proteins associated with meat products
   C. Tell the cook you are an inspector from the health department and ask what is in it
   D. Ask the cook for the recipe.

2. Which of the following is NOT a question you should ask before agreeing to an expensive remediation program for the clean-up of a chemical found at an industrial site?

   A. How much will is cost?
   B. What is the toxicity of the chemical?
   C. What will the land be used for?
   D. You should ask all of these questions and many more.

3. Which of the following is NOT an example of a critical thinking question?

    A. What is the definition of pollution?
    B. What concepts are central to my thinking about pollution?
    C. What assumptions am I making when I discuss pollution?
    D. How am I interpreting the information I have about pollution?

4. Which of the following is NOT part of an Environmental Impact Statement?

    A. Why the proposal is needed.
    B. Short-term and long-term effects of the project on the environment.
    C. How humans will benefit from the proposal
    D. Alternatives to the proposal.

5. Which of the following is NOT a step in a good decision-making process?

    A. Gather all relevant scientific information.
    B. Consider carefully and choose the best solution.
    C. Obtain a clear statement of the issue.
    D. Decide how many voters will support each course of action.

6. Which of the following statements is NOT true about the scientific method?

    A. A hypothesis is a prediction that can be tested.
    B. A hypothesis can be proven.
    C. A hypothesis can be disproven.
    D. A good experiment has controls.

7. In _____, estimated cost is compared with potential benefits to determine how much of a particular toxic chemical or pollutant society can tolerate.

    A. risk assessment
    B. cost-benefit analysis
    C. environmental impact statements
    D. ecological risk

8. Statement 1: Fish live in the water.
    Statement 2: Frogs live in the water.
    Conclusion based on _____ reasoning: Frogs are fish.

    A. deductive
    B. inductive

9. Which of the following is a global problem?

    A. The loss of wolves in Yellowstone.
    B. Oil spills in Kuwait.
    C. The hole in the ozone.
    D. The loss of wetlands in the Everglades.

10. The science of poisons is known as

    A. risk assessment.   C. carcinogenology.
    B. toxicology.   D. poison control.

11. Which of the following is NOT a problem when using mice to determine
    if a substance is carcinogenic?

    A. Mice often require higher doses of the substance than a human would normally be
       exposed to.
    B. It is difficult to extrapolate backwards from animal studies to human
       interpretations.
    C. The same mechanisms may not work in humans.
    D. It is hard to get large numbers of humans to volunteer for studies to determine if a
       substance causes cancer.

12. Estimating the risks involved in a particular action so that they can be compared
    and contrasted with other risks is known as

    A. cost-benefit analysis.   C. risk perception.
    B. risk management.   D. risk assessment.

13. Which risks tend to evoke the greatest fears in humans?

    A. Risks over which we have no control.
    B. Risks over which we have control.
    C. Risks that we choose to accept.
    D. Risks of which we are not aware.

14. The air conditioner in your 1987 Dodge Omni is broken. You take it to your auto
    repair shop and learn that the cost of replacement is going to be more than the
    car is worth. While talking to the mechanic, you learn that most of this cost is
    caused by the ban on CFCs. While doing some more research, you learn that
    this ban was instituted by Congress as a response to the reports of the hole in
    the ozone. Before writing to your Congresswoman, you need to learn more about

the issue. Which of the following sources would be the most reliable and least biased?

A. An Autoweek editorial on the poor quality of substitute molecules.
B. A local newspaper article on the hole in the ozone
C. An article in the journal *Science* by scientists measuring the effect of CFCs in the upper atmosphere.
D. An advertisement in the *National Inquirer*.

15. Which of the following is the best choice when considering the effects your answer to the question, "paper or plastic," will have on the environment?

A. Any choice you make has environmental consequences. The best you can do is make a rational decision about the type and amount of damage you do.
B. Always use renewable resources and you won't contribute to global warming.
C. Recycle plastic. It can be recycled countless times and will not end up in the landfill.
D. Dig up and transplant a living tree. This way there is no net gain or loss of a tree.

16. Risk =

A. perception of risk x exposure to risk
B. probability of risk x perception of exposure
C. probability of harm x probability of exposure
D. (birth rate - death rate)/100

17. The more verifiable _____ a hypothesis makes, the more valid the hypothesis is.
   A. assumptions   C. predictions
   B. conclusions   D. statements

18. Which of the following diseases or illnesses is examined most commonly when doing risk assessment on a potentially toxic chemical?

   A. cancer   C. birth defects
   B. reproductive disorders   D. viruses

19. Data are collected by

   A. observation and experimentation.
   B. inference and deduction.
   C. faith and intuition.
   D. analysis and interpretation.

20. Which of the following groups is the least prone to respiratory problems that are aggravated by air pollution?

   A. Infants
   B. Children, ages 2-6
   C. Young adults, ages 18-25
   D. Elderly people

21. The most common method of determining whether a chemical causes cancer is to

   A. Expose bacteria to low doses of the chemical and see whether or not they live.
   B. Expose laboratory animals to high doses of the chemical and see whether or not they develop cancer.
   C. Expose humans to high doses of the chemical and see whether or not they develop cancer.
   D. Expose humans to low doses of the chemical and see whether or not they develop cancer.

22. In 1989, epidemiologists in Germany established a direct link between cancer and a group of chemicals called _____. They observed the incidence of cancer in workers exposed to high concentrations of this chemical during an accident at a chemical plant in 1953, and found unexpectedly high levels of cancers of both the digestive and respiratory tracts.

   A. chlorofluorocarbons
   B. pesticides
   C. carbon dioxides
   D. dioxins

23. The _____ is responsible for tracking diseases.

   A. Food and Drug Administration
   B. National Disease Hotline
   C. American Medical Association
   D. Centers for Disease Control and Prevention

FILL IN:

1. The process of nutrient enrichment of freshwater lakes is well understood by ecologists, who call it _____ .

2. The possibility always remains that future evidence will require a _____ , a theory, or even a principle to be revised.

3. _____ is the plural form of datum.

4. Despite the wide range that often occurs between projected and actual costs, the "cost" portion of _____-_____ _____ is often easier to determine than are the health and environmental benefits.

5. Discovering general principles by the careful examination of specific cases is called _____ _____ .

6. _____ _____, which operates from generalities to specifics, adds nothing new to knowledge, but it can make relationships among data more apparent.

7. _____ is the study of compounds that are poisons.

8. The process that scientists use to answer questions or solve problems is called the _____ _____.

9. Much of the challenge of experimental science lies in designing a test that serves as a(n) _____, and in successfully isolating a single variable from all other variables.

10. Evaluation of an issue that includes the development and implementation of laws to regulate hazardous substances is known as _____ _____.

11. Chemical mixtures can interact by additivity, synergy, or _____ .

12. Many human endeavors may unintentionally contribute to outbreaks of infectious _____ .

13. When every herder in the village brings as many animals onto the commons as possible, the plants are killed from _____ , and the entire village suffers.

14. Legal and economic policies are needed to prevent the short-term degradation of our Earth's atmosphere, water, and other resources collectively called the _____ _____ .

15. A key step in the scientific method is to develop a(n) _____ , or educated guess, to answer the question.

16. The _____ requires that environmental impact statements be prepared to aid decision making about federally funded projects.

17. The number of students who die from sitting in a classroom with an asbestos ceiling is estimated at 0 per year. This number is the annual _____ _____.

18. Any factor that can influence the outcome of a process or experiment is called a _____ .

19. _____ is a systematic process to investigate the natural world.

20. Hypotheses are most useful when they make _____ that can be tested.

21. When nutrients are plentiful in a body of water, _____ can grow into filamentous mats that form a green scum over the surface of the water.

22. _____ are so well-established that the likelihood of their being rejected in the future is very small.

23. A(n)_____ _____ _____ assesses the effect a proposed project will have on the environment.

TRUE OR FALSE:

1. True   False   Scientists study a problem until they obtain a "final answer."

2. True   False   The "global commons" are those parts of our environment that are available to everyone but for which no single individual has responsibility---the atmosphere and the ocean, for example.

3. True   False   Attempting to extrapolate backward from data on the incidence of cancer in rats exposed to high levels of a substance to predict the incidence of cancer in humans exposed to trace amounts of that substance may not be scientifically sound.

4. True   False   Most environmental ills are inextricably linked to other persistent problems such as poverty, overpopulation, and social injustice, problems that are beyond the ability of a single nation to resolve.

5. True   False   Scientists admit that even the best risk assessments are based on assumptions that, if changed, could substantially alter the estimated risk.

6. True   False   Risks over which most of us have control, such as smoking or drinking, tend to evoke more fearful responses than risks over which we have no control.

7. True   False   Corporate estimates of the cost to control pollution are often many times higher than the actual cost turns out to be.

MAKING CONNECTIONS:

1. In the 1960s Lake Erie was declared dead. There were large algal blooms and many dead fish. Cultural eutrophication was the cause. (Look in Chapter 21 to define this process.) In Chapter 1, you read about the Zebra mussels that invaded the Great Lakes. These organisms are filter feeders and have caused the water clarity in the lake to improve dramatically. This means that there is a great reduction in the amount of plankton, including algae in Lake Erie. Why do the Zebra mussels affect water clarity? Is the introduction of a species such as the Zebra mussel a potential solution for bodies of water that suffer from cultural eutrophication.

PEOPLE WHO MATTER:

1. In 1950 Comita and Anderson observed that a filamentous cyanobacterium was growing in Lake Washington in large masses.

   a. Explain how they related this observation to the discharge of waste water into the lake.

   b. What is this process of aquatic nutrient enrichment called?

   c. Why is the increased growth of an organism like the cyanobacterium considered an environmental problem?

   d. What plan of action was implemented? Why did it take so long?

2. Garrett Hardin. Explain what Hardin meant when he described the "Tragedy of the Commons." Give an example of how we can interpret the word "commons" today and describe how individual desires compete with long-term goals.

MAKING DECISIONS:

1. List the types of questions that need to be addressed when trying to solve environmental problems.

2. List and define the 5 components of environmental problem solving.

3. Which risk assessment poses the highest risk, 4×10^{-3} or 4×10^{-9}? Why?

DOING SCIENCE:

1. What is the difference between a scientific theory and the use of the word theory in everyday life?

2. The students in Dr. Char's biology class read an advertisement that said that gardeners who use fertilizer brand Q will have plants that grow faster than plants grown without brand Q. Based on the claims in this advertisement, they decide to ask a question. They want to know "Do plants treated with brand Q grow faster than plants that are not treated with brand Q?" Their hypothesis is "Plants grown treated with brand Q will grow faster than plants not treated with brand Q."

    a. Rephrase their hypothesis into an IF... THEN statement.

    b. What prediction is made from the hypothesis?

    c. Design an experiment to test the hypothesis. Be sure to define which variables you will hold constant and which variable you will change. Explain how you will collect your data and how you might interpret the possible results.

CHECKING WHAT YOU KNOW (HINTS)

MULTIPLE CHOICE: (HINT)

1. B
2. D
3. A
4. C
5. D
6. B
7. B
8. B
9. C
10. B
11. D
12. D

13. A
14. C
15. A
16. C
17. C
18. A
19. A
20. C
21. B
22. D
23. D

FILL IN: (HINT)

1. eutrophication
2. hypothesis
3. Data
4. cost-benefit analysis
5. inductive reasoning
6. Deductive reasoning
7. Toxicology
8. scientific method
9. control
10. risk management
11. antagonism
12. disease

13. overgrazing
14. global commons
15. hypothesis
16. National Environmental Policy Act (NEPA)
17. death rate
18. variable
19. Science
20. predictions
21. cyanobacteria
22. Theories
23. environmental impact statement

TRUE AND FALSE: (HINT)

1. False
2. True
3. True
4. True

5. True
6. False
7. True

MAKING CONNECTIONS (HINT):

1. Cultural Eutrophication is the human-caused enrichment of nutrients in a body of water. These nutrients promote excessive growth of organisms such as cyanobacteria. When the algal blooms die, they start to decay, a process that uses up the available oxygen. If the oxygen is unavailable, the fish are unable to carryout aerobic respiration, and they too die.

Zebra mussels, being filter feeders, are able to ingest large quantities of plankton. They are so efficient at removing plankton, including algae, from the water that they are able to completely filter the water in the western basin of Lake Erie in one week. The reduced amount of plankton improves the clarity of the water. It makes it nice for people who don't wish to swim in green water, but it reduces the supply of available food for other desirable organisms.

Zebra mussels are NOT a potential solution to eutrophic bodies of water. Zebra mussels may be able to reduce the amount of algae and prevent the negative effects of cultural eutrophication, but they are exotic species. They compete with the native species and change the ecology of the environment into which they are introduced.

PEOPLE WHO MATTER (HINT):

1a. The growth of cyanobacteria requires an abundance of nutrients. Lake Washington was not previously known for high levels of nutrients. They traced the increase in nutrients to the discharge of waste water into the lake. They subsequently found other bacteria directly associated with polluted water, confirming their hypothesis.
b. This process of enrichment of the nutrients in water is called eutrophication.
c. This is a problem because as the bacteria die, they decay. The decay process uses up oxygen. The lack of oxygen makes it harder for other species to survive. They decay process can also smell.
d. Nutrient rich waste water was diverted. Public disbelief in the problem and resistance to paying the cost to solve the problem are two reasons it took so long. .

2. The term the commons is based historically on the tradition of sharing a common space for grazing animals owned by individual members of the community. According to Hardin, the commons system works well as long as the individuals respect the commons. When individuals get greedy, graze more animals than the commons can support, the commons are damaged and everyone is harmed. Today, we interpret the commons to represent the common resources such as air and water. Just as with the commons of old, an individual's consumption of the resources in the commons has an impact on the suitability of the commons for everyone. An individual who wastes resources or pollutes for short term benefit can impair long-term sustainability.

MAKING DECISIONS: (HINT)

1. *How is information pertinent to the problem gathered?*
At what point can scientific data be considered certain enough to act on the problem?
Who makes the decisions about how to solve the problem?
What are the pros and cons of each potential solution?

2. *Scientific assessment. The process of gathering all of the relevant scientific information available. Often this means doing novel experiments or creating models to try to understand the basis of the problem.*

Risk analysis. Using scientific information to assess the potential effects of action versus inaction.

Public education. Explaining the problem, possible solutions, and potential effects to the general public.

Political action. Making and implementing a decision by using the political process.

Follow-through. Ongoing assessment of the actions taken and their impact on the problem.

3. *4×10^{-3} This number is written in scientific notation. If you write it out it is 0.004. To figure this out:*

Write the number 4 on a blank line
   4.0
Move the decimal place 3 places to the left.

0 004.0 and you get the number 0.004.
   ^

4×10^{9} is 0.000000004 when you move the decimal place 9 spaces to the left. This is a much smaller number than 0.004. Therefore it represents far less risk.

DOING SCIENCE: (HINT)

1. *A scientific theory is generally agreed upon by the scientific community because it is supported by a large body of scientific evidence. The common usage of the word theory implies a guess. People often believe that when you use the word theory, anyone's guess is as good as anyone else's. This is not true with a scientific theory. It must be supported by lots of evidence before it is generally accepted.*

2. a. *If plants are treated with brand Q, then they will grow faster.*
b. *They predict that plants will grow faster if treated with brand Q.*

c. *The variable they will change will be the amount of brand Q given to each plant. They must control for all other factors including type of plant, soil, light, water... They should measure the plant growth on a regular basis. If plants treated with Q grow larger than untreated plants, the data support the hypothesis. If the treated plants do not grow larger, the hypothesis should be revised. If the data are inconclusive, the experiment should be revised and repeated.*

CHAPTER 3 -- ECOSYSTEMS AND ENERGY

LEARNING THE LANGUAGE:

abiotic
algae
aquatic ecosystems
atmosphere
bacteria
biomass
biosphere
biotic
carbohydrate
carnivore
cell
cell respiration
chemical energy
community
consumer
decomposers
detritus
ecosphere
ecosystem
energy
energy flow
entropy
environment
first law of thermodynamics
food

food chain
food web
gross primary productivity
herbivore
inorganic
kinetic energy
krill
lithosphere
mechanical energy
multicellular organism
net primary productivity
omnivore
ozone
photosynthesis
population
potential energy
primary consumers
pyramid of biomass
pyramid of energy
pyramid of numbers
salinity gradient
saprotrophs
second law of thermodynamics
species
trophic level

CHECKING WHAT YOU KNOW:

MULTIPLE CHOICE:

1. The following diagram represents the loss of _____ as you move up the food chain.

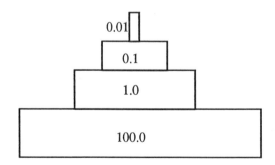

A. species   B. predators   C. herbivores   D. energy

2. Which form of energy flows as charged particles?

    A. electrical energy   C. mechanical energy

    B. nuclear energy   D. potential energy

3. Wh... ... ...n to another, some useful energy is usually lost in the

... ...sents the actual path of energy in your lunch of a fish

    ... gae

    ... ---> perch

    ... --> perch ---> human

... ...rm to another, some energy is lost.

    B. Matter must be recycled.

    C. All energy comes from the sun.

    D. Energy can not be created or destroyed.

6. Why is an herbivore able to extract energy from the environment more efficiently than a carnivore.

    A.   There is little loss of energy as you move up the energy pyramid. Therefore, a carnivore is really as efficient as an herbivore.

    B.   Most of the energy is lost as you move up the energy pyramid. The plants capture solar energy and the herbivore eats the plants, getting more of the original energy from the sun than the carnivore.

    C.   Protein is the important thing to observe when looking at food chains. There is more protein in meat than in plants.

    D.   Actually, it is the decomposers who can get the best energy conversion because they are eating dead stuff.

7. $C_6H_{12}O_6 + 6O_2 + 6 H_2O \text{ -----> } 6CO_2 + 12H_2O + energy$
   This is the equation for

   A. photosynthesis
   B. cell respiration

   C. primary net productivity
   D. biomass

8. An organism that is able to make its own food is a

   A. producer
   B. consumer

   C. detritivore
   D. decomposer

9. Plants are able to make their own food. They do this through photosynthesis. They are

   A. producers
   B. consumers

   C. carnivores
   D. omnivores

10. A food web represents all of the interconnected _____ in an ecosystem.

    A. food chains
    B. ecospheres

    C. limiting factors
    D. competitions

11. A pride of lions in the forest in Oz is an example of a(n)

    A. community
    B. population

    C. ecosystem
    D. biosphere

12. The most efficient transfer of energy to the highest trophic level of a food chain is represented by which of the following examples?

    A. corn --> cattle --> human
    B. corn --> human
    C. bee --> clover --> cattle --> human
    D. algae --> minnow --> trout --> human

13. The following diagram represents an energy pyramid. Which level (A,B,C, or D) represents the energy of the primary consumers?

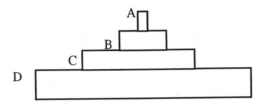

14. Which of the following terrestrial ecosystems averages the greatest net primary productivity?

A. Temperate grassland
B. Savanna

C. Temperate deciduous forest
D. Northern coniferous forest

15. _____ break down plant and animal and waste materials to obtain food to respire for energy.

A. Consumers
B. Producers
C. Decomposers
D. All of these organisms require plant and animal waste materials.

16. Virtually all energy on Earth comes from

A. coal.
B. nuclear isotopes.

C. geothermal.
D. the sun.

17. Which of the following organisms found in a salt marsh in the Chesapeake Bay is NOT a consumer?

A. mosquito
B. clapper rail

C. cordgrass
D. meadow vole

18. Can you have an energy pyramid in a pond?

A. yes

B. no

19. Which of the following is NOT a consumer?

    A. fungus
    B. nematode

    C. mouse
    D. black bear

20. Which type of energy comes from within atomic nuclei?

    A. chemical energy
    B. radiant energy

    C. heat energy
    D. nuclear energy

21. Photosynthesis uses energy to produce food. Respiration burns food to release energy. Given these two statements, which of the following statements is NOT TRUE?

    A. Plants carry out photosynthesis.
    B. Animals carry out respiration.
    C. Plants do not carry out respiration.
    D. Animals do not carry out photosynthesis.

22. A rabbit eats black raspberries and other plants. The rabbit is a(n)

    A. decomposer
    B. herbivore

    C. carnivore
    D. omnivore

23. Members of a(n) _____ are able to reproduce with one another, and their offspring are reproductively viable.

    A. community
    B. ecosphere

    C. habitat
    D. species

24. Which diagram represents the greatest amount of entropy?

    A   B   C   D

25. All of the lions, tigers, and bears in the forest on the way to Oz make up a(n)

    A. organism
    B. population

    C. community
    D. ecosystem

26. All of the lions, tigers, bears, and yellow bricks in the forest on the way to Oz make up a(n)

    A. organism
    B. population

    C. community
    D. ecosystem

27. $CO_2 + H_2O + sunlight ------> Glucose (food) + oxygen$

    This is the formula for

    A. decomposition
    B. respiration

    C. photosynthesis
    D. hydrogen sulfide metabolism

28. An ecological pyramid is a graphic representation of the relative _____ levels in a food chain.

    A. respiration
    B. energy
    C. primary productivity
    D. heat

29. First and second laws of thermodynamics govern

    A. the flow of energy.
    B. species interactions.
    C. food chains.
    D. essentially all interactions in the ecosphere.

30. Which of the following is NOT a correct food chain?

    A. grass ---> cow ---> human
    B. mouse ---> seed ---> snake ---> owl
    C. algae ---> zooplankton ----> zebra mussel ---> shell crushing fish
    D. weed ---> grasshopper ---> bird

FILL IN:

1. $6CO_2 + 12H_2O + $ radiant energy $----> C_6H_{12}O_6 + 6H_2O + 6O_2$ is the chemical equation for _____.

2. The _____ (nonliving, or physical) environment includes such physical factors as temperature, sunlight, and precipitation.

3. Consumers that eat producers are called primary consumers, which usually means that they are exclusively _____ (plant eaters).

4. The chemical energy of food is released and made available for biological work by the process of _____ _____ .

5. Microbial decomposers feed on the components of dead organisms and organic wastes, degrading them into simple _____ materials that can then be used by producers to manufacture more organic material.

6. Animals that use the bodies of other organisms as a source of food energy and body-building materials are _____.

7. The _____ _____ _____ of an ecosystem is the rate at which organic matter is produced by photosynthesis.

8. The _____ is the soil and rock of earth's crust.

9. _____ make important elements (such as potassium, nitrogen, and phosphorus) found in dead organisms available for use by new generations of organisms.

10. A _____ is a group of similar organisms whose members freely interbreed with one another in the wild and do not interbreed with other sorts of organisms.

11. Who eats whom in an ecosystem, or the path of energy flow, occurs in _____, in which energy from food passes from one organism to the next in a sequence.

12. A(n) _____ _____ _____ illustrates the energy content, often expressed as kilocalories per square meter, of the biomass of each trophic level in an ecosystem.

13. A(n) _____ consists of all the populations of different species that live and interact together within an area.

14. Scientists are concerned that the _____ hole over Antarctica could possibly damage the algae that form the base of the food web in the southern ocean.

15. The _____ is the gaseous envelope surrounding the earth.

16. The _____ encompasses the biosphere and its interactions with the atmosphere, hydrosphere, and lithosphere.

17. _____ _____ _____ is the amount of biomass that remains in plant tissue after plant cellular respiration. It represents the rate at which organic matter is incorporated into plant tissues.

18. Secondary and tertiary consumers are flesh-eating _____ that eat other animals.

19. Plants are the most significant producers on land, whereas _____ and certain types of bacteria are important producers in aquatic environments.

20. Producers provide both _____ and oxygen for the rest of the community.

21. _____ and fungi are important examples of decomposers.

22. The most productive _____ _____ are algal beds, coral reefs, and estuaries.

23. At the simplest level, atoms are organized into molecules, which are organized into _____ in living organisms.

24. Cells are organized into tissues, tissues into organs, organs into body systems, and body systems into individual _____ _____.

25. A(n) _____ is a more inclusive term than community because it is a community together with its physical environment.

26. The environment consists of two parts, the _____ (living) environment, which includes all organisms, and the nonliving, or physical, environment, which includes such physical factors as temperature, sunlight, and precipitation.

27. A(n) _____ _____ is a complex of interconnected food chains in an ecosystem. It is a realistic model of the flow of energy and materials through ecosystems

28. In photosynthesis, plants absorb the radiant energy of the sun and convert it into the chemical energy contained in the bonds of _____ molecules.

29. A(n) _____ _____ _____ illustrates the total biomass at each successive trophic level.

30. The remains of dead organisms, called _____, provide food for many inhabitants of salt marshes and bays.

31. _____ is a measure of disorder or randomness.

32. The _____ is the Earth's supply of water-- liquid and frozen, fresh and salty.

33. All of earth's communities of organisms are organized into the _____ .

34. A(n) _____ _____ _____ shows the number of organisms at each trophic level in a given ecosystem.

35. The _____ _____ _____ states that as each energy transformation occurs, some of the energy is changed to heat energy that is then given off into the cooler surroundings.

36. Organized, usable energy has a low entropy. _____, which is a disorganized form of energy, has a high entropy.

37. Producers, or _____, are the photosynthetic organisms that are at the base of almost all food chains; they include plants, algae, and some bacteria.

38. Virtually all of Earth's organisms depend on the sun for _____.

39. _____ are tiny shrimplike organisms that eat algae in the Antarctic food web.

40. _____ are microbial heterotrophs that break down organic material and use the decomposition products to supply themselves with energy.

41. The photosynthetic pigment _____ is green and absorbs radiant energy.

42. Consumers that eat producers are called _____ _____.

43. A gradual change from unsalty fresh water to salty ocean water which occurs in places such as the Chesapeake Bay is called a _____ _____.

44. Stored energy is _____ _____.

45. All of the nonliving, or physical, components of the environment are _____.

46. _____ _____ is the energy stored in the chemical bonds of molecules.

47. _____ eat a variety of things including producers and consumers.

48. The passage of energy in a one-way direction through an ecosystem is know as
_____ _____.

49. _____ is a quantitative estimate of the total mass of living material in an ecosystem.

50. Energy in the movement of matter is called _____ _____.

51. Each link in a food chain is referred to as a _____ _____.

TRUE OR FALSE:

1. True   False   Nutrients such as nitrates and phosphates promote the growth of producers.

2. True   False   Ecology is the narrowest field in biology because it encompasses such a limited number of disciplines.

3. True   False   Generally speaking, the more net primary productivity a region has, the greater the biodiversity of the region.

4. True   False   Humans consume the least amount of natural resources of any species on the planet.

5. True   False   Food webs are short because of the dramatic increase in energy content that occurs at each trophic level.

6. True   False   The most productive terrestrial ecosystems on the planet are tropical rain forests.

7. True   False   Food chains are a more accurate picture of the flow of energy in an ecosystem than food webs.

8. True   False   Organisms obey the laws of thermodynamics like everything else in the universe.

9. True   False   Autotrophs carry out photosynthesis, whereas producers only use cell respiration.

10. True   False   Net primary productivity is always less than gross primary productivity.

PEOPLE WHO MATTER:

1. Who is F. Sherwood Roland?

2. What was his hypothesis?

3. What had to occur between 1974 and 1987 that caused Roland's hypothesis to become widely accepted?

4. What are the implications of a thinning ozone layer?

MAKING CONNECTIONS:

1. Describe the connection between the Antarctic food web and an increase in the amount of ultraviolet radiation reaching the algae in the oceans around Antarctica.

MAKING DECISIONS:

1. How can an energy pyramid be used to support the decision to be a vegetarian?

2. People in developing countries consume less protein than Americans. Furthermore, essentially all of their protein comes from grains. In the United States, most of the protein consumed is as meat, yet the per capita consumption of grain is much higher here. Why is this the case?

DOING SCIENCE:

1. You are part of a team of scientists observing a meadow that contains a rare species of mole. The community would like to build a much needed hospice at this site. You would like to be able to move the moles to another site. Come up with a plan that will help you decide if the move can be successful.

CHECKING WHAT YOU KNOW: (HINT)

MULTIPLE CHOICE: (HINT)

1. D	9. A	17. C	25. C
2. A	10. A	18. A	26. D
3. D	11. B	19. A	27. C
4. D	12. B	20. D	28. B
5. D	13. C	21. C	29. D
6. B	14. C	22. B	30. B
7. B	15. C	23. D	
8. A	16. D	24. D	

FILL IN: (HINT)

1. photosynthesis
2. abiotic
3. herbivores
4. cell respiration
5. inorganic
6. consumers
7. gross primary productivity
8. lithosphere
9. Decomposers
10. species
11. food chains
12. pyramid of energy
13. community
14. ozone
15. atmosphere
16. ecosphere
17. Net primary productivity
18. carnivores
19. algae
20. food
21. Bacteria
22. aquatic ecosystems
23. cells
24. multicellular organisms
25. ecosystem
26. biotic
27. food web
28. carbohydrate
29. pyramid of biomass
30. detritus
31. Entropy
32. hydrosphere
33. biosphere
34. pyramid of numbers
35. second law of thermodynamics
36. Heat
37. autotrophs
38. energy
39. Krill
40. saprotrophs (or decomposers)
41. chlorophyll
42. primary consumers
43. salinity gradient
44. potential energy
45. abiotic
46. chemical energy
47. Omnivores
48. energy flow
49. Biomass
50. mechanical energy
51. trophic level

TRUE OR FALSE: (HINT)

1. True
2. False
3. True
4. False
5. False

6. True
7. False
8. True
9. False
10. True

PEOPLE WHO MATTER: (HINT)

1. F. Sherwood Roland and Mario Molina first described the chemical reactions that occur in the stratosphere between chlorofluorocarbons and ultraviolet radiation, thereby depleting the ozone layer.

2. Roland hypothesized that CFCs in the stratosphere would react with ultraviolet radiation and ozone, thereby causing the break down of ozone.

3. Many scientists did many experiments in the laboratory to confirm that the chemical reactions could occur. They also found ways to make observations in the stratosphere that provided data to support the hypothesis. The key observation was the discovery of a thinning in the ozone layer over the Antarctic in 1987.

4. As the ozone layer thins, more ultraviolet radiation reaches the surface of the planet. Ultraviolet radiation has lots of energy and can cause damage to molecules such as DNA, the molecule responsible for heredity in living organisms. DNA damage can lead to cancers and genetic defects.

MAKING CONNECTIONS: (HINT)

1. Algae are producers. They form the base of the energy pyramid in this ecosystem. If ultraviolet radiation is able to damage the algal populations, then the gross primary productivity and the net primary productivity of the ecosystem will be reduced. The region will be able to support fewer numbers of organisms.

MAKING DECISIONS: (HINT)

1. The closer you are to consuming producers, the more energy that is transferred. As you move up the trophic levels, which occurs when you eat meat, more energy is lost. As with any change in diet or exercise, you should consult your physician before you make such a decision. Vegetarians must be well-informed to ensure that they consume the appropriate amounts of all essential foods, particularly some amino acids.

2. Consuming meat puts humans as secondary consumers in the food chain. Energy is lost in feeding the animals that become the meat.

DOING SCIENCE: (HINT)

1. You will need to figure out where the mole fits into to food web in this meadow and whether the same web exists in the new meadow. What does the mole eat? What eats it? You will also need to figure out where the mole lives, how it finds mates...

Once you have done a comparison of the two habitats, you need to transport a few moles to the new meadow and track them to see if they survive.

CHAPTER 4 -- ECOSYSTEMS AND LIVING ORGANISMS

LEARNING THE LANGUAGE:

algae

bacteria

coevolution

commensalism

community

competition

competitive exclusion

ecological niche

ecosystem

ecotone

edge effect

epiphytes

eukaryotic

evolution

food

fundamental niche

habitat

host

interspecific competition

keystone species

limiting factor

mutualism

mycorrhizae

natural selection

overproduction

parasite

parasitism

pathogen

pioneer community

population

predation

predator

prey

primary succession

realized niche

secondary succession

species

species diversity

succession

symbiosis

warning coloration

zooxanthellae

CHECKING WHAT YOU KNOW:

MULTIPLE CHOICE:

1. Your habitat is where you live. Your _____ is what you do there.

    A. job

    B. role

    C. ecological niche

    D. competition

2. Dwarf mistletoe grows on the branches of the lodgepole pine tree. This interaction, where one species benefits and the other is harmed, is called

    A. parasitism

    B. symbiosis

    C. mutualism

    D. competition

3. Why do certain katydids resemble leaves in color and in the pattern of veins on their wings?

    A. They eat trees with similar leaves.
    B. They are plants that are able to fly.
    C. They avoid predation with this camouflage.
    D. This warns experienced predators away.

4. Why is a fundamental niche larger than a realized niche?

    A. Realized niches are the space and resources available to a species.
    B. Other organisms occupy parts of the fundamental niche preventing the species from using all the resources it has the potential to use.
    C. A fundamental niche represents all the potential aspects of an organism's existence that are necessary for survival, and reproduction.
    D. Neither the realized niche or the fundamental niche are actually occupied by the species.

5. Which of the following is a pathogen?

    A. silverfish
    B. crown gall bacterium

    C. mycorrhizae
    D. *Rhizobium* bacterium

6. Members of a(n) _____ are able to reproduce with one another, and their offspring are reproductively viable.

    A. community
    B. ecosphere

    C. habitat
    D. species

7. The first species to populate an area that has been disrupted by a forest fire are called _____.

    A. nursemaid plants
    B. pioneer species

    C. climax communities
    D. primary succession

8. What is biodiversity?

    A. The rain forest in Costa Rica.
    B. The number of different species found in an area or on the planet.
    C. The number of threatened species found on the planet
    D. The number of habitats found in an area or on the planet.

9. No two species can occupy the same ecological niche at the same time in the same place indefinitely. This is the

A. law of tolerance.
B. second law of thermodynamics.
C. competitive exclusion principle.
D. first law of thermodynamics

10. The following graph shows the number of fish that survive versus the pH of the pond. You can see that there is a pH where the most fish are able to survive. This is the _____ pH for these fish.

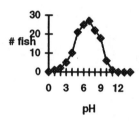

A. minimal   B. optimal   C. tolerable   D. maximal

11. A bear eats a salmon. The salmon is

A. lunch.
B. the prey.
C. an herbivore.
D. the predator.

12. Which of the following is NOT a premise on which Charles Darwin based his theory of evolution by natural selection?

A. Each species produces more offspring than will survive.
B. Individuals within a species exhibit heritable variations.
C. Organisms best suited to survival will reproduce and pass their traits on to the next generation.
D. Organisms within a population change in response to changes in their environment.

13. Where is community complexity the greatest?

A. At the margins of adjacent communities.
B. In an isolated community.
C. Where one species dominates a community.
D. Where the community is relatively new.

14. A bear eats a salmon. The bear is

A. lunch.
B. the prey.
C. an herbivore.
D. the predator.

15. The _____ species to enter an area that has been disturbed by cultivation or fire are called pioneer species.

   A. first
   B. second

   C. intermediate
   D. last

16. The dark circles represent the ecological niche of the brown anole. The lighter circles represent the ecological niche of the green anole. Which of the following diagrams represents the overlap between these species?

   A.
   B.
   C.

17. Species on an island are said to be _____ because of the difficulty in reaching and colonizing the island.

   A. geographically isolated
   B. naturally selected

   C. competitively excluded
   D. reproductively assimilated

18. A rare species of orchid requires minute traces of the element molybdenum. It can only grow in areas that have more than 5ppm of molybdenum. Molybdenum is the _____ for this orchid.

   A. ecological niche
   B. limiting factor

   C. optimum
   D. tolerance limit

19. Which process takes the least amount of time?

   A. Evolution
   B. Primary succession
   C. Secondary succession

20. Which of the following animals can be found at ALL stages of succession in a North Carolina abandoned field?

   A. cottontail rabbit
   B. white-tailed deer

   C. short-tailed shrew
   D. white-footed mouse

21. What is the BEST way to maintain biodiversity and/or help conserve a species?

   A. Encourage habitat preservation.
   B. Try to save each species individually.

C. Don't worry about individual species. New ones will evolve to take their place.
D. Stop logging.

22. Which of the following would NOT be common during the first two years of secondary succession?

A. crabgrass
B. horseweed

C. oak sapling
D. ragweed

23. A monarch butterfly selects milkweed pods and consumes them. The monarch butterfly is an example of a(n)

A. parasite   B. host   C. predator   D. virus

24. The difference between primary and secondary succession is that primary succession

A. results in a climax community
B. starts with the formation of soil from bare rock
C. causes a community to change over time
D. occurs after a farmer stops plowing his field

25. Which of the following is NOT a plant adaptation to avoid predation?

A. thorns
B. flight

C. protective chemicals
D. leathery leaves

26. Soybean plants and other legumes require less nitrogen fertilizer because they have a _____ relationship with a bacterium that fixes nitrogen and makes it available to the plant.

A. saprophytic
B. mutualistic

C. competitive
D. parasitic

FILL IN:

1. The interdependent evolution between two interacting species is called _____.

2. A symbiotic relationship in which both partners benefit is called _____.

3. _____ cells have a high degree of internal organization, containing such organelles as nuclei, chloroplasts (in photosynthetic cells), and mitochondria.

4. Species compete with one another for _____, water, living space, and other resources.

5. _____ are small plants that grow attached to the bark of a tree.

6. The first organisms to colonize (or recolonize) an area make up the _____ _____.

7. _____ have a prokaryotic cell structure: they lack a nuclear envelope and other internal cell membranes.

8. A(n) _____ is an association of different populations of organisms that live and interact together in a given environment.

9. Darwin's mechanism of evolution by _____ _____ consists of four observations about the natural world: overproduction, variation, limits on population growth, and survival to reproduce.

10. The local environment in which an organism lives is its _____ .

11. Symbiotic algae, which are called _____, live inside cells of coral animals, where they photosynthesize and provide carbon and nitrogen compounds as well as oxygen.

12. _____ _____ is ecological succession in an environment that has not previously been inhabited.

13. The potential ecological niche of an organism is its _____ _____, whereas the niche an organism actually occupies is it's realized niche.

14. A biological community and its abiotic environment together comprise a(n) _____.

15. _____ is a symbiotic relationship in which one partner -- the parasite -- obtains nutrients t the expense of the other -- the host.

16. _____ _____ is ecological succession in an environment that has previously been inhabited.

17. The niche an organism actually occupies is its _____ _____.

18. The _____ _____ represents the totality of an organism's adaptations, its use of resources, and the lifestyle to which it is suited.

19. Symbiosis is the result of _____, the interdependent evolution between two interacting species.

20. The change in species composition produced in a(n)_____ is known as the edge effect.

21. Within an ecosystem, _____ _____ help determine the species composition and functioning of the entire ecosystem.

22. Environmental factors that actually determine an organism's realized niche can be extremely difficult to identify. These are the _____ _____.

23. Symbiotic _____, called zooxanthellae, live inside cells of the coral, where they photosynthesize and provide the animal with carbon and nitrogen compounds as well as oxygen.

24. Every organism is thought to have its own role within the structure and function of an ecosystem; we call this role its _____.

25. Parasitism is a symbiotic relationship in which one partner -- the parasite -- obtains nutrients at the expense of the other -- the _____.

26. _____ is a type of symbiosis in which one organism benefits and the other one is neither harmed nor helped.

27. The process of community development over time, which involves species in one stage being replaced by different species, is called _____.

28. Many ecologists think that no two species can occupy the same niche in the same community for an indefinite period of time because _____ _____ occurs.

29. _____ is any intimate relationship or association between two different species.

30. A change in species composition at the edge of ecotones is called the _____ _____.

31. _____ is defined as the number of species present in area or ecosystem.

32. Each species produces more offspring than will survive. This is called _____.

33. All of the members of a species that live in a defined area is a _____.

34. A(n) _____ obtains nutrients at the expense of its host.

35. Some organisms have _____ _____ to alert experienced predators to avoid eating them.

36. Members of the same _____ are able to breed with one another and produce offspring that are fertile.

37. A parasite that causes a disease is called a _____.

38. _____ is the consumption of one organism by another.

39. _____ are the mutualistic associations between fungi and the roots of plants.

40. Two different species of paramecia living in the same pond require the same nutrients. These paramecia are said to be in _____ _____ with one another.

TRUE OR FALSE:

1. True   False   No two species can occupy the same space indefinitely.

2. True   False   A realized niche is larger than a fundamental niche.

3. True   False   In a mutualistic relationship, both species benefit.

4. True   False   Predation is the consumption of one species by another species.

5. True   False   An ecotone contains all the habitats of the adjacent ecosystems.

6. True   False   The microcosm created by a NASA scientist only requires sunlight and water to continue to thrive in balance.

7. True   False   Secondary succession occurs after a volcano covers the land with lava.

8. True   False   Evolution can be defined as a change in the genetic makeup of a population that occurs over time.

9. True   False   Species diversity is directly related to the environmental stress of a habitat.

PEOPLE WHO MATTER:

1. Explain the experiment performed by P.F. Gause that provided the first evidence for the competitive exclusion principle.

2. Two species of fish, one native and the other introduced, survive in what seem to be identical niches in Florida. Why don't scientists use this as evidence to disprove the competitive exclusion principle?

MAKING CONNECTIONS:

1. Draw an energy pyramid for the following community members. Describe the interactions among the various species.

Lichens live on rocks.
Caribou eat lichens and moss.
Wolves eat caribou.

MAKING DECISIONS:

1. You have discovered the last known populations of blue-footed spelunks living in three caves in the Ozarks. You wish to devise a conservation plan for this endangered species. You would like to try to introduce populations of this species into other caves in the area. Conservation of this species will be extremely expensive. What information do you need to have to decide if a conservation plan is feasible and whether it should be implemented?

DOING SCIENCE:

1. Zebra mussels (Chapter 1) entered the Great Lakes in the late 1980's. Assume you are an aquatic ecologist studying native clams in a remote bay that has not been infested with this organism. List some research questions you might ask about this ecosystem.

2. Choose one of your questions from #1 and design an experiment to try to answer it. Be sure to include your hypothesis and the appropriate controls. Remember, you are working with a species that has already been shown to outcompete native species elsewhere. Think about how you will prevent the further spread of the organism.

CHECKING WHAT YOU KNOW: (HINT)

MULTIPLE CHOICE: (HINT)

1. C	8. B	15. A	22. C
2. A	9. C	16. C	23. C
3. C	10. B	17. A	24. B
4. B	11. B	18. B	25. B
5. B	12. D	19. C	26. B
6. D	13. A	20. C	
7. B	14. D	21. A	

FILL IN: (HINT)

1. coevolution
2. mutualism
3. Eukaryotic
4. food
5. Epiphytes
6. pioneer community
7. Bacteria
8. community
9. natural selection
10. habitat
11. zooxanthellae
12. primary succession
13. fundamental niche
14. ecosystem
15. Parasitism
16. Secondary succession
17. realized niche
18. ecological niche
19. coevolution
20. ecotone
21. keystone species
22. limiting factors
23. algae
24. ecological niche
25. host
26. Commensalism
27. succession
28. competitive exclusion
29. Symbiosis
30. edge effect
31. Species diversity
32. overproduction
33. population
34. parasite
35. warning coloration
36. species
37. pathogen
38. Predation
39. Mycorrhizae
40. interspecific competition

TRUE OR FALSE: (HINT)

1. True	4. True	7. False
2. False	5. False	8. True
3. True	6. False	9. False

PEOPLE WHO MATTER: (HINT)

1. Gause grew two species of paramecium separately in test tubes. The populations displayed typical growth curves. When he put both species in the same tube, one thrived and the other died out.

2. Organisms require many different things for survival. Not only do they require obvious things like nesting space and food, but they also require trace minerals, specific levels of humidity or sun... Many of these essential items are difficult to identify. Therefore, when two species seem to thrive in the same ecological niche, scientists suspect that the niches vary in some yet-to-be identified way.

MAKING CONNECTIONS: (HINT)

1.

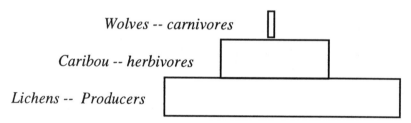

Wolves -- carnivores

Caribou -- herbivores

Lichens -- Producers

MAKING DECISIONS: (HINT)

1. What is the cost of this research? Where are the caves? What are the human impacts of spreading the species? -- Do they carry disease? Does the species serve a practical function in cave ecocystems? Food? Medicine? Aesthetics? Is it a keystone species? What is the cost of expanding its habitat? Where will this money come from? What other conservation projects are competing for these funds? Do the benefits of conservation outweigh the costs, and how will you convince the general public that this is true?

DOING SCIENCE: (HINT)

1. Why haven't the zebra mussels entered this bay? Is there something about this region that has kept them out? What will be the affect of the zebra mussel on the native clams? How much do their ecological niches overlap? Will there be a sufficient realized niche for the native clams to survive? What will be the impact of this organism on the food chain?

2. *Is there something about this bay that hasn't allowed zebra mussels to colonize it? There are a couple of hypotheses. Not enough human traffic to spread them. The flow of water into the bay from a river is sufficient to keep the veligers (young mussels). The chemical composition of the bay prevents colonization by the zebra mussels.*

IF the chemical composition of the bay has prevented zebra mussels from colonizing it, THEN water taken from the bay should impair the growth of some developmental stage of zebra mussels.

Take water samples from around the bay. Put these samples in aquaria (arranged in such a way as to prevent the inadvertent release of mussels). Add zebra mussels in different stages of development and observe their survival rates.

CHAPTER 5 -- ECOSYSTEMS AND THE PHYSICAL ENVIRONMENT

LEARNING THE LANGUAGE:

altitude
ammonification
assimilation
atmosphere
bacteria
biogeochemical cycle
carbon cycle
cell respiration
climate
coal
combustion
Coriolis effect
denitrification
desert
energy
evaporation
exosphere
fault
fossil fuels
Gaia hypothesis
groundwater
gyre
heterocysts
hydrologic cycle
infrared radiation
inorganic
latitude
lava

magma
mesosphere
nitrification
nitrogen cycle
nitrogen fixation
ozone
phosphorus cycle
photosynthesis
phytoplankton
plankton
plate tectonics
prevailing winds
protein
radiation
rain shadow
runoff
seismic waves
stratosphere
subduction
thermosphere
transpiration
tropical cyclone
troposphere
ultraviolet radiation
upwelling
watershed
weather
wind

CHECKING WHAT YOU KNOW:

MULTIPLE CHOICE:

1. The majority of sunlight that reaches the Earth's outer atmosphere

    A. is absorbed by the atmosphere.
    B. runs the water cycle.
    C. is captured by photosynthesis.
    D. drives the winds and ocean currents.

2. In the following diagrams, the circle represents the Earth. The parallel lines represent sunlight reaching the surface of the planet. Which diagram represents the least intensity of light reaching the surface?

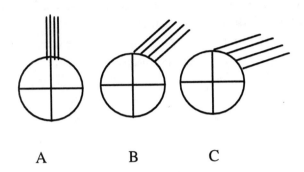

   A   B   C

3. _____ is the most common gas in the atmosphere.

   A. Carbon dioxide   C. Oxygen
   B. Neon   D. Nitrogen

4. Energy _____ the biosphere and matter _____.

   A. moves through, must be recycled   C. must be recycled, moves through it
   B. moves through, moves through it   D. must be recycled, must be recycled

5. My friend Martin is flying a dollar store kite from the top of a nearby hill. The kite is in the

   A. troposphere   C. bathosphere
   B. stratosphere   D. thermosphere

6. Which climate zone experiences the lowest temperatures?

   A. polar   B. mild   C. continental   D. tropical

√ 7. If you add up the amount of water that falls on the land and the amount of water that evaporates from the ocean, you see a net gain of water on the land surface and a net loss of water from the ocean. Why aren't the oceans shrinking as the land gets wetter?

    A. The last statement in the question is not true. The ocean is shrinking, and the land is getting wetter. This is because the hole in the ozone is getting bigger and letting more energy reach the surface of the planet.

    B. Actually the reverse process is happening. The ocean is getting fuller and fuller and the land is getting drier. There is more coastal flooding and more droughts than ever. It is raining less on the land, and evaporation from the ocean is decreasing.

    C. The numbers used to calculate rainfall are determined by measuring the amount of rain that is collected in detectors at weather stations. There are far more weather stations on the land than there are anywhere in the ocean. This means that the data are biased in favor of finding rainfall on the land and missing it on the ocean. If we had better data, the global water budget would probably balance.

    D. The water that falls on the land runs off the surface in rivers and ultimately ends up in the ocean. Since more runs off than percolates into the soil or is retained in rivers, lakes, and reservoirs, the global water budget can be balanced.

8. _____ occur where fresh water meets saltwater near the coast.

    A. Estuaries
    B. Watersheds
    C. Hydrologic cycles
    D. Groundwaters

9. Meteors appear in the:

    A. stratosphere
    B. mesosphere
    C. thermosphere
    D. exosphere

10. Generate(s) circular ocean currents called gyres?

    A. Currents
    B. Variations in seawater density
    C. Prevailing winds
    D. Coriolis effects

√11. A biogeochemical cycle is the

    A. movement of energy between the biological, chemical, a geological realms.
    B. loss of energy from the biological, chemical, a geological realms.
    C. movement of matter between the biological, chemical, a geological realms.
    D. conversion of food to energy.

12. Which of the following processes removes carbon dioxide from the atmosphere?

    A. photosynthesis
    B. cell respiration
    C. combustion
    D. condensation

13. What happens to the electromagnetic radiation that enters the atmosphere from the sun?

    A. It is reflected.   C. It is absorbed.
    B. It is scattered.   D. All of these answers are correct.

14. _____ is/are the site of long-term carbon storage

    A. Trees   C. Ocean phytoplankton
    B. Carbon dioxide   D. Fossil fuels

15. *Rhizobium* bacteria live inside nodules in the roots of some types of plants. They provide nitrogen to the plant. This is an example of:

    A. competition   C. mutualism
    B. parasitism   D. predation

16. Which of the following statements best describes the movement of materials through the biosphere?

    A. Energy can neither be created nor destroyed.
    B. Energy passes through the biosphere; everything else must be recycled.
    C. Whenever you convert energy from one form to another, some useful energy is lost as heat.
    D. No two molecules can occupy the same niche indefinitely.

17. Which of the following statements best describes the movement of energy through the biosphere?

    A. Energy can neither be created nor destroyed.
    B. Energy passes through the biosphere; everything else must be recycled.
    C. Whenever you convert energy from one form to another, some useful energy is lost as heat.
    D. No two molecules can occupy the same niche indefinitely.

18. Which of the following is NOT a way that water gets from the surface of the planet to the atmosphere?

    A. transpiration   B. evaporation   C. precipitation

19. _____ water holds more dissolved oxygen than _____ water.

    A. Cold, warm   B. Warm, cold

20. Long-term storage of phosphorus occurs in

    A. fossil fuels.   C. the atmosphere.
    B. rocks and sediments.   D. trees.

21. Virtually all energy on earth comes from

    A. coal.   C. geothermal.
    B. tidal power.   D. the sun.

22. Which climate zone experiences the highest temperatures?

    A. dry   B. mild   C. continental   D. tropical

23. Which of the following is NOT a step in the nitrogen cycle?

    A. nitrification   C. cell respiration
    B. ammonification   D. assimilation

24. In the continental United States, prevailing winds come off the Pacific Ocean and move eastward. Which city is in a rain shadow?

    A. Denver, Colorado   C. Portland, Oregon
    B. San Francisco, California   D. San Diego, California

25. Why is phosphorus important biologically?

    A. It is a component of tree bark.
    B. It is leached into the environment through exposed rock.
    C. It is a key element in DNA and ATP.
    D. It is denitrified by bacteria.

26. _____ returns carbon to the atmosphere.

    A. Photosynthesis   C. Combustion
    B. Assimilation   D. Erosion

27. What is the nitrogen cycle?

    A. A biochemical pathway.
    B. A new mountain bike with a nitrogenous frame.
    C. An atomic clock based on the cycling of nitrogen from bacteria to the atmosphere.
    D. The movement of nitrogen between the biotic and abiotic components of the biosphere.

28. Which of the following is NOT true of the nitrogen cycle?

    A. Nitrogen is directly involved in photosynthesis and cell respiration.
    B. A large sink (storage site) for biologically unavailable nitrogen is the atmosphere.
    C. Nitrogen fixation and nitrification occur before atmospheric nitrogen becomes biologically available (particularly to plants).
    D. Nitrogen is an important component of DNA and proteins.

29. Which of the following is a funnel of air associated with thunderstorms?

    A. cyclone   B. hurricane   C. typhoon   D. tornado

30. _____ is the description of the physical conditions of the atmosphere.

    A. Climate   C. Humidity
    B. Weather   D. Temperature

31. Which of the following processes converts nitrogen from its biologically active forms to forms unusable by most living organisms?

    A. nitrogen fixation   C. denitrification
    B. assimilation   D. ammonification

32. Look at figure 5-20. Which two plates share a convergent boundary?

    A. African and South American   C. Indian-Australian and Eurasian
    B. Indian-Australian and Antarctic   D. Nazca and Pacific

33. When energy is converted from one form to another, some useful energy is lost, usually in the form of heat. This is the

A. law of tolerance
B. competitive exclusion principle
C. first law of thermodynamics
D. second law of thermodynamics

34. Photosynthesis uses energy produce food. Cell respiration burns food to release energy. Given these two statements, which of the following statements is NOT TRUE?

A. Plants carry out photosynthesis.
B. Animals carry out respiration.
C. Plants do not carry out respiration.
D. Animals do not carry out photosynthesis.

35. The Louisiana Purchase encompassed all of the land drained by the Mississippi River. This is an example of a(n)

A. aquifer
B. river bed
C. estuary
D. watershed

36. The nitrogen cycle is dependent on _____ that carry out the processes of nitrification and denitrification.

A. photosynthetic algae
B. plants
C. bacteria
D. factories

37. _____ is the process that allows water to enter the atmosphere by passing into the roots of plants and out through the leaves.

A. Transpiration
B. Evaporation
C. Condensation
D. Precipitation

38. Which of the following elements does NOT have an important component of its biogeochemical cycle in the atmosphere?

A. nitrogen
B. oxygen
C. carbon
D. phosphorus

39. In the following diagrams, the circle represents the Earth. The parallel lines represent sunlight reaching the surface of the planet. Which diagram represents the greatest intensity of light reaching the surface?

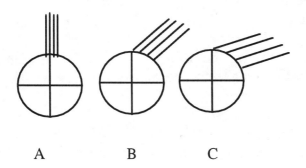

A   B   C

FILL IN:

1. The conversion of biological nitrogen compounds into ammonia is known as _____.

2. The stratosphere 2 to 28 miles above the earth's surface and contains a layer of _____ that is critical to life because it absorbs much of the sun's damaging ultraviolet radiation.

3. The area of land being drained by runoff from a specific area is called a _____ .

4. The series of hypotheses that Earth's organisms adjust the environment to improve conditions for life has been called, collectively, the _____ .

5. The _____ _____ has no biologically important gaseous compounds.

6. _____ , the loss of water vapor from land plants, adds water to the atmosphere.

7. Plant roots absorb either nitrate (NO_3) or ammonia (NH_3) that was formed by nitrogen fixation and nitrification, and incorporate the nitrogen of these molecules into plant proteins and nucleic acids. This incorporation process is called _____.

8. The sun's _____ is the product of a massive nuclear fusion reaction.

9. The atmosphere exhibits complex horizontal movements called winds that result in part from differences in atmospheric pressure and from the rotation of the Earth, called the _____ _____.

10. _____ tend to blow from areas of high atmospheric pressure to areas of low pressure, and the greater the difference between the high- and low-pressure areas, the stronger they are.

11. The conversion of ammonia (NH_3) to nitrate (NO_3^-) is called _____.

12. The overall equation for _____ is:
    light + 6CO$_2$ + 12H$_2$O ----------> C$_6$H$_{12}$O$_6$ + 6O$_2$ + 6H$_2$O

13. The _____ , which extends from 80 to 500 kilometers (50 to 310 miles), is characterized by steadily rising temperatures.

14. C$_6$H$_{12}$O$_6$ + 6O$_2$ + 6H$_2$O ----------> 6CO$_2$ + 12H$_2$O + ENERGY for biological work
    This equation represents how carbon dioxide is returned to the atmosphere by the process of _____ _____ .

15. The movement of Earth's crustal plates is called _____ _____ .

16. Temperature increases with increasing altitude in the _____ because the absorption of ultraviolet radiation by the ozone layer heats the air.

17. _____ develop in the rain shadows of mountain ranges or in continental interiors.

18. Prevailing winds generate circular oceanic currents called _____ .

19. While the atmosphere protects the Earth from high-energy radiation, it allows visible light and some _____ _____ to penetrate, and they warm the surface and the lower atmosphere.

20. Magma that reaches the surface of the Earth is called _____ .

21. In places in the mantle, the rock reaches the melting point, forming pockets of molten rock called _____ .

22. _____ _____ the first step in the nitrogen cycle is the conversion of gaseous nitrogen (N$_2$) to ammonia (NH$_3$).

23. Coastal _____ along the south American coast provides nutrients for large numbers of phytoplankton, which in turn support a complex food web.

24. When two plates grind together, one of them sometimes descends under the other, in a process known as _____ .

25. The temperature of the troposphere decreases with increasing _____ by about -6°C for every kilometer.

26. The _____ _____ continuously renews the supply of water that is so essential to life and involves an exchange of water among the land, the atmosphere, and living organisms.

27. Energy, released as _____ _____, or vibrations that spread through the rocks rapidly in all directions, causes one of the most powerful events in nature, an earthquake.

28. Carbon in coal, oil, natural gas, and wood can be returned to the atmosphere by the process of _____ .

29. A _____ _____ is a giant, rotating tropical storm with high winds.

30. _____ converts nitrate to nitrogen gas.

31. Water enters the atmosphere by _____ and transpiration, and leaves the atmosphere as precipitation.

32. The movement of water from land to ocean is called _____ ,

33. The _____ , the layer of atmosphere directly above the stratosphere, extends from 45 to 80 kilometers (28 to 50 miles) above the Earth's surface.

34. The sun's energy is emitted into space in the form of electromagnetic _____ -- especially visible light and infrared and ultraviolet radiation.

35. Weather, including turbulent wind, storms, and most clouds, occurs in the _____ .

36. Water percolates, or seeps, downward through the soil and rock to become _____ .

37. The _____ that use nitrogenase must insulate the enzyme from oxygen because nitrogenase functions only in the absence of oxygen.

38. The global movement of carbon between the abiotic environment, including the atmosphere, and organisms is known as the _____ .

39. Ultimately, all absorbed solar _____ is radiated into space as infrared (heat) radiation.

40. The absorption of _____ _____ by the ozone layer heats the air, and so temperature increases with increasing altitude in the stratosphere.

41. _____ _____ carbon-containing compounds formed from the remains of ancient organisms, are the end products of photosynthesis that occurred millions of years ago.

42. Plants assimilate nitrate, producing _____ and nucleic acids in the process.

43. _____ comprises the average weather conditions that occur in a place over a period of years.

44. Most earthquakes occur along _____ or fractures in the crust along which rock moves forward and backward, up and down, or from side to side.

45. The _____ is an invisible layer of gases that envelops the earth.

46. The persistent _____ _____ blowing over the ocean produce mass movements of surface oceanic water known as currents.

47. The outermost layer of the atmosphere, the _____ , begins about 500 kilometers (310 miles) above Earth's surface.

TRUE OR FALSE:

1. True   False   The atmosphere becomes less dense as it extends outward into space; most of its mass is found near the Earth's surface.

2. True   False   Photosynthesis removes carbon dioxide from the abiotic environment and incorporates it into biological molecules.

3. True   False   Nitrogenase only functions in the presence of oxygen.

4. True   False   The sun makes life on Earth possible.

5. True   False   Prevailing winds blow strongly, but only occasionally.

6. True   False   The El Nino can alter both ocean and atmospheric circulation patterns.

7. True   False   Most volcanic activity is caused by the movement of crustal plates.

8. True   False   Cyclones and hurricanes are two different types of storms with very different characteristics.

9. True   False   Climate is the average weather a region experiences.

10. True   False   Clouds form when the moisture in the air reaches the saturation point.

MAKING CONNECTIONS:

1. In 1996, scientists at the Goddard Space Flight Center proposed that humans may have altered the rotation of the Earth's axis and that the North Pole may have moved as much as 2 feet. Combine this hypothesis with the evidence for a hole in the ozone over Antartica (chapter 20). How could these two effects interact to affect the surface of the planet?

MAKING DECISIONS:

1. Your read in your local paper that a large cattle feedlot has been proposed for your area. Explain to your neighbors how phosphate from Florida can end up in the ocean through this feedlot.

2. What is the potential impact of nitrogen and phosphate in the wastes on your local river?

3. How will you decide whether or not you support construction of a feedlot in your area?

DOING SCIENCE:

1. Your text describes the El Nino-Southern Oscillation (on pages 94—96). During an El Nino, populations of certain fish such as anchovies decline. Populations of shrimp and scallops can thrive. Pick one of these populations and design an experiment or set of experiments to determine how the El Nino affects that population.

CHECKING WHAT YOU KNOW: (HINT)

MULTIPLE CHOICE: (HINT)

1. A	11. C	21. D	31. C
2. C	12. A	22. D	32. C
3. D	13. D	23. C	33. D
4. A	14. D	24. A	34. C
5. A	15. C	25. C	35. D
6. A	16. B	26. C	36. C
7. D	17. B	27. D	37. A
8. A	18. C	28. A	38. D
9. C	19. A	29. D	39. A
10. C	20. B	30. B	

FILL IN: (HINT)

1. ammonification
2. ozone
3. watershed
4. Gaia hypothesis
5. phosphorus cycle
6. Transpiration
7. assimilation
8. energy
9. Coriolis effect
10. Winds
11. nitrification
12. photosynthesis
13. thermosphere
14. cell respiration
15. plate tectonics
16. stratosphere
17. Deserts
18. gyres
19. infrared radiation
20. lava
21. magma
22. Nitrogen fixation
23. upwelling
24. subduction
25. altitude
26. hydrologic cycle
27. seismic waves
28. combustion
29. tropical cyclone
30. Denitrification
31. evaporation
32. runoff
33. mesosphere
34. radiation
35. troposphere
36. groundwater
37. bacteria
38. carbon cycle
39. energy (or radiation)
40. ultraviolet radiation
41. Fossil fuels
42. proteins
43. Climate
44. faults
45. atmosphere
46. prevailing winds
47. exosphere

TRUE OR FALSE: (HINT)

1. *True*	4. *True*	7. *True*	10. *True*
2. *True*	5. *False*	8. *False*	
3. *False*	6. *True*	9. *True*	

MAKING CONNECTIONS: (HINT)

1. Review hole in the ozone. The ozone hole caused by the presence of chlorofluorocarbons in the stratosphere catalyzing the breakdown of ozone. Ozone chemistry in the stratosphere absorbs ultraviolet radiation, preventing it from reaching the surface of the planet, where it can damage tissues and organisms. A change in the rotation axis of the Earth could change the intensity of radiation reaching the surface in a given region. It could also shift the regions being exposed to the ultraviolet radiation, which could affect different populations.

MAKING DECISIONS: (HINT)

1. Phosphate-rich rock is mined in Florida and made into fertilizer. The fertilizer is spread over cornfields where it becomes incorporated into the corn. The cattle in the feedlot are fed the corn. Phosphate wastes from the feedlot and from the meat packing facility can end up in the local river, which will eventually flow out to the ocean (Atlantic or Pacific, depending on which side of the Continental Divide you live.) Furthermore, waste from humans who consume the meat will also end up in the rivers and will also flow to the ocean.

2. Refer to chapters 2 and 21. Look up cultural eutrophication. Nitrogen and phosphorus are essential to plant growth on land. Thus they are used as fertilizers. Excess nitrogen and phosphorus in the water also act as fertilizers, causing algae to grow. Large algal blooms can decay, using up the available oxygen and causing the asphyxiation of other organisms such as fish. The decaying algae also contribute to a foul odor.

3. First, list out all of the reasons for supporting the feedlot. Then make a list of the reasons to oppose the feedlot. Balance out the costs and benefits. Remember, your decision will have to be made based on your own moral, ethical, cultural, and religious beliefs, and you should consider your own financial reality. The following table presents some of the possibilities.

support feedlot	*oppose feedlot*
improve local economy	*smell bad*
more jobs -- one for me?	*water pollution*
improve roads to area	*more truck traffic*

DOING SCIENCE: (HINT)

1. Pick one population. Make a testable hypothesis. For example, the El Nino causes scallop populations to boom because they are bottom dwellers, and when the El Nino prevents upwelling the nutrients stay where the scallops can get them. A testable hypothesis would be:

a. "If scallops are given a steady supply of nutrients, then the population will thrive".
Grow scallops in the lab in nutrient-rich and nutrient-deprived tanks.
b. If El Nino prevents upwelling then the nutrient levels near the bottom should remain the same or increase during an El Nino event.

Measure nutrient levels before, during, and after an El Nino event.

CHAPTER 6 -- MAJOR ECOSYSTEMS OF THE WORLD

LEARNING THE LANGUAGE:

algae	Mediterranean climate
allelopathy	nekton
alpine tundra	neritic province
altitude	oceanic province
annuals	pelagic environment
arctic tundra	permafrost
atmosphere	perennials
atoll	phytoplankton
barrier reef	plankton
benthic environment	profundal zone
benthos	runoff
biome	salinity
bloom	salt marsh
boreal forest	savanna
chaparral	source
delta	spring turnover
desert	standing-water ecosystem
estuary	surface water
euphotic zone	swamp
fall turnover	taiga
flood plain	temperate deciduous forest
flowing-water ecosystem	temperate grassland
food web	temperate rain forest
freshwater wetlands	terrestrial
fringing reef	thermal stratification
intertidal zone	thermocline
limnetic zone	tropical rain forest
littoral zone	tundra
mangrove forest	wetlands
marine snow	zooplankton
marsh	zooxanthellae

CHECKING WHAT YOU KNOW:

MULTIPLE CHOICE:

1. Which of the following features is NOT used to classify a biome?

   A. type of soil
   B. the climate

   C. plants and animals that live there
   D. the depth of the water

2. The _____ is the northernmost biome and is characterized by permafrost, low-growing vegetation and an extremely short growing season.

A. tundra

B. taiga

C. temperate grassland

D. benthos

3. A _____ is usually small, shallow, cold, and swift.

A. meander

B. tributary

C. headwater stream

D. river mouth

4. In which environment are all the organisms predators or scavengers?

A. neritic province

B. euphotic province

C. oceanic province

D. pelagic province

5. Which of the following is a characteristic of desert plants?

A. adapted to eliminate excess water

B. adapted to conserve water

C. adapted to live in fertile soil

D. adapted to hibernate during cold winters

6. Which of the following is NOT a characteristic of the taiga?

A. coniferous trees

B. south of the tundra

C. short growing season

D. permafrost throughout

7. Which organism is NOT likely to be found in a temperate deciduous forest?

A. bird

B. oak tree

C. cactus

D. mouse

8. Which of the following is NOT a reason why estuaries are biologically important?

A. They are nutrient rich and very productive.

B. They hold little life other than decomposers.

C. They provide a nursery for aquatic organisms.

D. They are the transition between freshwater and saltwater ecosystems.

9. The following diagram shows a volcanic island surrounded by coral. This is the first stage in the formation of a(n) _____ after the island sinks below sea level.

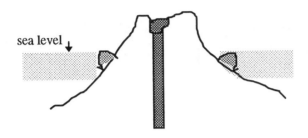

A. barrier reef

B. fringing reef

C. atoll

D. tropical reef

10. Which of the following organisms is NOT likely to be found in the coniferous biome of Yellowstone?

A. ponderosa pine

B. elk

C. bear

D. penguin

11. In the San Francisco Estuary, 2% of the land is riparian woods that supports 50% of the species of wildlife found in the entire estuary. Farmland, which takes 60% of the total land area in the estuary, only supports 20% of the wildlife. Increasing the amount of riparian woods to 4% of the estuary would allow it to support 100% of the wildlife.

In the previous statement there are several facts and an inference. Which of the following statements is the inference?

A. Riparian woods make up 2% of the estuary.

B. Riparian woods support 50% of the wildlife.

C. Doubling the amount of riparian woods would double the number of species it can support.

D. Farmland is not a naturally occurring part of the estuary.

12. The following diagram represents a temperate lake in?

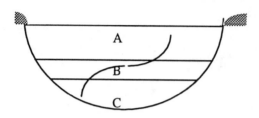

A. spring   B. summer   C. winter   D. fall

13. Which of the following is NOT considered a biome?

A. Pond   B. Tundra   C. Savanna   D. Desert

14. Which of the following has the greatest effect on biome distribution in tropical regions?

A. temperature
B. precipitation

C. light
D. longitude

15. One difference between a temperate rain forest and a temperate deciduous forest is

A. the temperature.
B. types of trees.

C. latitude.
D. length of growing season.

16. Marine snow is

A. organic debris that drifts into the oceanic province.
B. a winter storm in the oceanic province.
C. human debris that drifts into the oceanic province.
D. a winter storm that originates over the oceanic province.

17. Which of the following is NOT a characteristic of the oceanic province?

A. dark
B. cold

C. high pressure
D. nutrient rich

19. _____ is responsible for bringing nutrients up from the bottom of the lake and for oxygenating the deep water.

   A. the water cycle
   B. spring turnover

   C. the hydrologic cycle
   D. nutrient recycling

20. Which of the following is NOT a zone found in standing water ecosystems?

   A. littoral   B. nektonic   C. limnetic   D. profundal

21. In the following diagram of a temperate lake, which region represents the thermocline?

FILL IN:

1. Alpine tundra typically lacks permafrost and receives more precipitation than
   _____ _____ .

2. Rocky shore intertidal _____ (seaweeds) usually have thick, gummy coats, which dry out slowly when exposed to air, and flexible bodies not easily broken by wave action

3. Important environmental differences exist between high _____ and high latitudes that affect the types of organisms found in each place.

4. _____ are plants that live for more than two years.

5. _____ are plants that complete their life cycles in one growing season.

6. Desert plants are noted for _____ , an adaptation in which toxic substances secreted by roots or shed leaves inhibit the establishment of competing plants nearby.

7. At higher altitudes where the climate is very cold, a kind of tundra occurs, with vegetation composed of grasses, sedges, and small tufted plants; it is called _____ _____ to distinguish it from arctic tundra.

8. The _____ is a layer of permanently frozen ground.

9. In _____ _____ the summers are hot, the winters are cold, and the rainfall is uncertain.

10. The _____ is where a flowing water ecosystem begins.

11. An algal _____ is a temporary population explosion that usually occurs in the spring and fall.

12. A circular coral reef that surrounds a central lagoon is called a(n) _____.

13. The _____ _____ is part of the open ocean that overlies the ocean floor at depths greater than 200 meters.

14. _____ _____ _____ are characterized by mineral-poor soils, and very high rainfall all year long.

15. A large relatively distinct terrestrial region with characteristic climate, soil, plants, and animals is called a(n) _____.

16. Lands that are transitional between freshwater and terrestrial ecosystems are usually covered by shallow water. These regions are called _____ _____.

17. _____ is characterized by permafrost, extreme cold, and a short growing season.

18. _____ are small or microscopic organisms carried about by the currents.

19. The _____ is a tropical grassland with widely scattered clumps of low trees. It has seasonal or low rainfall and prolonged dry periods.

20. _____ _____ are characterized by mild winters with abundant rainfall and dry summers.

21. _____ is the concentration of dissolved salts, which affects the kinds of organisms present in aquatic ecosystems.

22. A _____ _____ which is the tropical equivalent of a salt marsh, covers 70% of tropical coastlines.

23. A river is an example of a(n) _____ _____ _____.

24. In the _____ _____ _____ sufficient light to support photosynthesis penetrates to about 150 meters.

25. Free floating algae and cyanobacteria make up the _____, the producers in aquatic ecosystems.

26. The _____ _____ is the deepest part of the lake where no light reaches.

27. _____ are dry areas found in both temperate and tropical regions. They are subject to temperature extremes even in 24 hour periods.

28. A(n) _____ is a coastal body of water, partly surrounded by land, with access to the open ocean. It is supplied with fresh water from rivers.

29. _____ are organisms that are large and strong swimmers.

30. Most organisms in the oceanic provence depend on _____ _____, the organic debris that falls into their region from above.

31. Eleven percent of Earth's land is covered in _____ which is characterized by extremely cold winters, little precipitation, a short growing season, and soil that is acidic and mineral-poor.

32. In temperate lakes, _____ _____ or the layering of water, is caused by the penetration of sunlight which warms the water.

33. The _____ _____ is a shallow-water area along the shore of a lake or pond. Plants like cattails grow here.

34. All of the open ocean region is referred to as the _____ _____.

35. Land that is covered by shallow fresh water for at least part of the year and has water-tolerant vegetation is called _____ _____.

36. _____ _____ are coral reefs in shallow warm water that are directly attached to the shore of an island.

37. The abrupt temperature transition in a temperate lake is called the _____.

38. The area of shore between low and high tides is the _____ _____.

39. The autumnal mixing of waters in temperate lakes is called _____ _____.

40. The ocean floor is the _____ _____.

41. A(n) _____ _____ is separated from land by open water. It forms after the volcano on the island becomes inactive and starts to erode.

42. _____ are photosynthetic algae that live symbiotically with coral in coral reefs.

43. The _____ _____ is open water away from lakeshore where sunlight is able to penetrate.

44. The biome located in extreme northern regions with long winters, short summers, and all day sun is the _____ _____.

45. Organisms that dwell in the benthic environment are referred to as _____.

46. _____ are freshwater wetlands that are dominated by grasses.

47. The open ocean that stretches from the shore to ocean depths of 200 meters is called the _____ _____.

48. Lakes and ponds are examples of _____ _____ _____.

49. _____ _____ _____ occur in temperate areas where precipitation ranges from 30-50 inches and the soil is loaded with organic material. Oak, hickory, and beech trees are found in these regions.

50. A freshwater wetland that has trees and shrubs is called a(n) _____.

TRUE OR FALSE:

1. True False The tropical rain forest has a canopy that allows light to penetrate to the forest floor.

2. True False Mangrove forests grow in tropical and subtropical coastal regions.

3. True False Careful planning will allow the eventual restoration of the Florida Everglades their original form.

4. True False Coral reefs have high species diversity and low productivity.

5. True False Light penetrates to the tropical rain forest floor at riverbanks.

6. True   False   The Everglades is an ecosystem that we have fully defined and understand completely.

7. True   False   Temperature and precipitation influence the distribution of organisms.

8. True   False   Wetlands provide habitat for migratory birds.

9. True   False   Temperature has the greatest influence on species composition in aquatic ecosystems.

10. True   False   In higher latitudes, temperature has a greater effect on species composition than precipitation.

MAKING CONNECTIONS:

1. Humans have a great need for water. Consider only the true human need for sufficient water to support life. For the purposes of this question, do not worry about the effect of pollution. In which biome(s) will the human need for water and for access to water have the least negative impact on the environment?

2. You are participating in a leadership seminar. Your final test is to keep your team alive in a remote wilderness area. You are allowed to pick the biome where you and your team will be dropped off. Which biome do you believe you will be most likely to survive? What are the obstacles you will encounter? What are the materials and supplies you need to have to survive here? (Assume you can only take what will fit into a 35 pound backpack, and only a small amount of emergency food can be included.)

MAKING DECISIONS:

1. Page 124 contains a Focus On segment that discusses the Florida Everglades. Read this section carefully and then list all of the groups who have a say in the management of this region along with their goals or needs.

2. What do you think about the price supports for the sugar crop?

DOING SCIENCE:

1. The following web site contains information about the biosphere 2 project.
       http://www.bio2.com/index.html
(There are numerous others. To find them, type biosphere into your search engine.)
Biosphere 2 is a large structure in the Arizona desert that can be almost completely self-contained. Plants and animals from a variety of biomes have been brought to the facility

to attempt to recreate the conditions of the biome in a controlled environment. The biomes represented include desert, marsh, ocean, rain forest, savanna, and intensive agriculture. The following excerpt from this web page describes some student research in the rainforest ecosystem. Read it carefully and then design an experiment you would carry out if you were a student studying in the Biosphere 2 for a semester.

"Research during 1996 directed by James Wetterer, Columbia University, showed that the crazy ant (*Paratrechina longicornis*) dominates the animal community of Biosphere 2, creating a situation very similar to highly-disturbed tropical islands. Sugary excretions from plant-feeding bugs (Order Homoptera) seem to be an important food source for ants. Homopteran diversity seems to be high and may be favored by the presence of crazy ants. Students are participating in follow-up projects to verify and extend this research on crazy ant biology." (http://www.bio2.com/research/bmgproj.htm)

2. There is currently a push to put a human on the planet Mars. This would involve an extended voyage in a spaceship. What lessons could be learned from Biosphere 2 that could help in planning the mission to Mars?

CHECKING WHAT YOU KNOW: (HINT)

MULTIPLE CHOICE: (HINT)

1. D	8. B	15. B
2. A	9. C	16. A
3. C	10. D	17. D
4. C	11. C	18. B
5. B	12. B	19. B
6. D	13. A	20. B
7. C	14. B	

FILL IN: (HINT)

1. arctic tundra
2. algae
3. altitude
4. Perennials
5. Annuals
6. allelopathy
7. alpine tundra
8. permafrost
9. temperate grasslands
10. source
11. bloom
12. atoll
13. oceanic provence
14. Tropical rain forests
15. biome
16. freshwater wetlands
17. Tundra
18. Plankton
19. savanna
20. Mediterranean climates
21. Salinity
22. mangrove forest
23. flowing-water ecosystem
24. euphotic zone
25. phytoplankton

26. profundal zone
27. Deserts
28. estuary
29. Nekton
30. marine snow
31. taiga or boreal forest
32. thermal stratification
33. littoral zone
34. pelagic environment
35. freshwater wetlands
36. Fringing reef
37. thermocline
38. intertidal zone
39. fall turnover
40. benthic environment
41. barrier reefs
42. Zooanthellae
43. limnetic zone
44. arctic tundra
45. benthos
46. Marshes
47. neritic province
48. standing-water ecosystems
49. Temperate deciduous forests
50. swamp

TRUE OR FALSE: (HINT)

1. false
2. true

3. false
4. false

5. *true*
6. *false*
7. *true*

8. *true*
9. *false*
10. *true*

MAKING CONNECTIONS: (HINT)

1. You may first expect that the human need for water and for access to water would have the least impact in biomes that receive the greatest amounts of water, regions such as tropical and temperate rain forests. One might also think about how a human would gain access to water in a rain forest. Could the act of moving toward the streams and rivers in a rain forest cause more harm than the similar process in a deciduous forest?

2. Select a biome. Think about climate, precipitation, availability of water, availability of food, temperature, etc... Obstacles include all of these things as well as the types of organisms in the environment, including disease organisms. For materials you will need to think of how you will obtain food, how will you protect your team from the elements and how you will protect yourselves from the native species.

MAKING DECISIONS: (HINT)

1.

Group	goals/needs
environmentalists	restoration
tourism industry	restoration, maintain a place for tourists to visit, maintain access to area by tourists
developers	need land for development, need reason for people to move there, flood control, drinking water and other resources
sugar industry	land for farming, ability to use farming practices (fertilizers, pesticides) to obtain crop, maintain price support
government	Serve constituents, keep jobs, get funding for projects, get funding for re-election, balance the costs with the benefits.
citizens	living conditions, water quality, personal beliefs
commercial fishing	damage to fish populations

2. Balance what you know about the effect of sugar production on the Everglades with the economic benefits to the region of jobs in the industry. Investigate the reason price supports exist. Make up your own mind.

DOING SCIENCE: (HINT)

*1. **State a hypothesis.** For example, "Removal of crazy ants from a portion of the biosphere will result in less diversity in the homopteran population in that region." **Design the experiment.** Isolate a region in the rain forest biome and remove all of the* *crazy ants. What problems could you encounter while trying to do this? (Making sure all the ants have been removed. Keeping them out of the area.) What will you collect as data? (Number of hompteran species.) How will you collect your data? (Count organisms. Think about sampling techniques.)* **What will be your control?** *(Collect the same data on a region as similar as possible that contains crazy ants.)*

2. How to produce food in a sealed environment. How to manage biomes. What the biological consequences of changing oxygen and carbon dioxide concentrations are. How humans behave when confined for long periods of time.

CHAPTER 7 -- ECONOMICS, GOVERNMENT, AND THE ENVIRONMENT

LEARNING THE LANGUAGE:

coal-burning power plant
command and control
consumer
economics
ecosystem
emission charge
emission reduction credit
emission charge policy
Endangered Species Act
external cost
habitat

marginal cost
marginal cost of pollution
marginal cost of pollution abatement
National Environmental Policy Act
natural resources
optimum amount of pollution
pollution control
population
sulfur dioxide
unfunded mandate
waste-discharge permit

CHECKING WHAT YOU KNOW:

MULTIPLE CHOICE:

1. Command and control regulation of pollution involves

    A. prevention of any pollution.
    B. blocking the building of businesses or industries that cause pollution.
    C. cleaning pollution up after it has been generated.
    D. setting limits on levels of pollution.

2. In a(n) _____ the price of goods are determined by supply and demand.

    A. economic market
    B. free market

    C. marketplace
    D. external market

3. Some poor countries have overexploited their natural resources in an attempt to

    A. destroy their environment as quickly as possible.
    B. raise their gross domestic products as quickly as possible
    C. make their leaders wealthy.
    D. reduce the marginal cost of pollution.

4. While it is easy to determine the cost of _____ in terms of property damage and medical expense, it is difficult to estimate a real cost for its effect on the environment.

A. species extinction
B. pollution
C. natural resources
D. ecosystem development

5. A(n) _____ is a waste-discharge permit that can be bought and sold by companies producing emissions.

A. emission reduction credit
B. command and control permit

C. waste-discharge credit
D. marginal abatement credit

6. What legislative phrase made the difference between building a dam in Yosemite in 1913 and blocking the building of a dam in Dinosaur in the 1050s?

A. General revision
B. Antiquities preservation

C. Without impairment
D. Wise use

7. In what way are economists similar to scientists?

A. They have nothing in common.
B. They both experiment with other people's money.
C. They both make money, economists on the stock market, and scientists in the laboratory.
D. They both make hypotheses, test models, and analyze data.

8. At high pollution levels, the marginal cost of pollution abatement for each unit of pollution is:

A. low
B. moderately-priced

C. high
D. very high

9. In order to determine how much pollution can be allowed, we need to find a balance between a(n) _____ and an uninhabitable sewer.

A. uninhabited wilderness
B. inhabited sewer

C. human habitation
D. inhuman habitation

10. The _____ required coal-burning power plants to remove sulfur dioxide from their emissions with scrubbers.

A. Endangered Species Act
B. Clean Water Act
C. National Environmental Policy Act
D. Clean Air Act

11. There is a(n) _____ relationship between the marginal cost of pollution abatement and the amount of pollution.

A. inverse
B. reverse

C. linear
D. exponential

12. The _____ of eliminating one unit of pollution increases as more and more pollution is eliminated.

A. optimum level of pollution
B. marginal cost

C. external cost
D. emission control credit

13. Which of the following is NOT a flaw in the economic approach to pollution?

A. The true cost of environmental damage by pollution is difficult to determine.
B. The risks of unanticipated environmental catastrophe are not taken into account in assessing the potential environmental damage of pollution.
C. The root cause of the world's pollution problem is the failure to consider external costs in the pricing of goods.
D. A, B, and C are all flaws.

14. Which of the following is NOT a practice followed by a green hotel?

A. Use of cloth napkins.
B. Installation of low flow toilets.
C. Use of aerosols in cleaning products.
D. Use of recycled materials such as porcelain in roads.

15. Which of the following is NOT an example of a species that has been removed from the endangered species list?

A. American alligator
B. bald eagle

C. northern spotted owl
D. California gray whale

16. As the amount of pollution increases, the marginal cost of pollution _____ and the marginal cost of pollution abatement _____.

A. increases, increases
B. decreases, decreases

C. increases, decreases
D. decreases, increases

17. This environmentalist founded the Sierra Club.

   A. Theordore Roosevelt   C. Benjamin Harrison
   B. John Muir   D. Adam Werbach

18. This legislation, signed into law in 1970, revolutionized environmental protection in the United States.

   A. Endangered Species Act   C. National Environmental Policy Act
   B. Clean Water Act   D. National Environmental Education Act

19. This 1891 act, later rescinded, gave U.S. presidents the authority to establish national forests on public land.

   A. National Environmental Policy Act   C. National Forest Management Act
   B. Wildneress Act   D. General Revision Act

FILL IN:

1. When consumption or production of a product has a harmful side effect that is borne by people not directly involved in the market exchange for that product, the side effect is called a(n) _____ _____.

2. _____ is the study of how people use their limited resources to try to satisfy their unlimited wants.

3. As the human _____ has grown, its appetite for natural resources-- plants, animals, water, minerals, air, land, and so on-- has seriously stressed the Earth's environment.

4. Water and air _____ move readily across political borders.

5. The Clean Air Act of 1977 required coal-burning power plants to outfit their smokestacks with expensive "scrubbers" to remove _____ _____ from their emissions.

6. A government policy that controls pollution by issuing permits allowing the holder to pollute a given amount is called a _____ _____ _____ policy.

7. The web of relationships within an _____ is extremely complex and may be vulnerable to pollution damage, often with disastrous results.

8. Pollution control laws that work by setting pollution ceilings are called _____ _____ _____.

9. A government policy that controls pollution by charging the polluter for each unit of emissions, that is, by establishing a tax on pollution, is called a(an) _____ _____ _____ .

10. Ecosystem issues, such as evolution of biological diversity, biogeochemical cycles, and succession, are measured in centuries or even longer, whereas political time frames are measured in _____.

11. Goods, services, and money flow between businesses and _____ .

12. A waste-discharge permit that can be bought and sold by companies producing emissions is called a(n) _____ _____ _____.

13. Provisions of the Endangered Species Act require the government to protect the _____ of endangered species so that their numbers can increase.

14. The cost in environmental quality of a unit of pollution that is emitted into the environment is known as the _____ _____ _____ _____ .

15. Provisions of the _____ _____ _____ _____ require the generation of environment impact statements before development projects involving federal lands or funds can be started.

16. _____ _____ _____ _____ is the cost to dispose of a unit of pollution in a nonpolluting way.

17. States that protect their _____ _____ and have good environmental records have the best long-term prospects for economic development.

18. The optimum amount of pollution as the amount whose _____ _____ _____ _____ equals the marginal cost of pollution abatement (the point at which the two curves intersect).

19. A(n) _____ _____ is a law that is passed by the federal government that affects state or local governments but is not accompanied by the necessary federal funds to implement.

20. A(n) _____ _____ _____ _____ is the additional cost associated with one more unit of something.

21. The amount of pollution that is economically most desirable is the _____ _____ _____ _____.

22. A harmful side effect of production that is not reflected in a product's price is a(n) _____ _____.

23. A(n) _____ _____ is a tax on pollution.

TRUE OR FALSE:

1. True False The external cost of making a product is almost always included in the price.

2. True False It is difficult to measure the environmental cost of pollution.

3. True False As a result of environmental legislation, millions of acres of farmland that are vulnerable to soil erosion are no longer being farmed.

4. True False When the cost of pollution is zero, the opportunities to pollute are limited.

5. True False Economics and the environment are completely unrelated.

6. rue False The use without impairment clause of the law that established the National Park Service is the backbone of the legal protection afforded our national parks and monuments.

PEOPLE WHO MATTER:

1. Investigate the environmental contributions of John Muir.

2. How did President Theordore Roosevelt conserve natural resources in the United States?

3. Who in your community is involved in drafting or supporting environmental legislation? What issues are currently important for you and your neighbors?

MAKING CONNECTIONS:

1. You run a business that manufactures useful widgets for home consumption. You wish to take your corporation public. In order to attract investors, you want to make sure that you run a "green company." You package your widgets in minimal packaging using recycled materials. You have reduced your air and water pollution levels to below the EPA required levels. You use no toxic chemicals and generate no toxic waste. The production of useful widgets also generates a great deal of excess organic material. At the present time, you have no difficulty disposing of the organic material. You can dissolve it in water and send it down the drain or you haul it to the dump.

Why could sending the organic waste down the drain be a serious environmental problem?

What are the problems associated with sending your organic waste to the sanitary landfill?

MAKING DECISIONS:

1. Your local planning commission is debating a change in zoning laws that will permit you to construct your widget factory next door. Which environmental laws should you investigate if you wish to argue effectively about whether or not the factory should be built?

DOING SCIENCE:

1. A creative staff member has suggested that the organic waste from your widget factory could be dissolved in water and used as a fertilizer at a local tomato farm. Design an experiment to determine the effect of your organic waste on the tomato plants.

2. Your experiment is successful, and the tomato grower would like to use your widget water because it is cheaper than the traditional fertilizer. A local environmentalist protests the arrangement because widget water is a fertilizer that can get into the local surface and possibly groundwater supplies. What experiments can you do to test this?

CHECKING WHAT YOU KNOW: (HINT)

MULTIPLE CHOICE: (HINT)

1.	D	6.	C	11.	A	16.	C
2.	B	7.	D	12.	B	17.	B
3.	B	8.	A	13.	D	18.	C
4.	B	9.	A	14.	C	19.	D
5.	A	10.	D	15.	C		

FILL IN: (HINT)

1. external cost
2. Economics
3. population
4. pollution
5. sulfur-dioxide
6. waste-discharge permit
7. ecosystem
8. command and control
9. emission charge policy
10. years (or months)
11. consumers
12. emission reduction credit (ERC)
13. habitat
14. marginal cost of pollution
15. National Environmental Policy
16. marginal cost of pollution abatement
17. natural resources
18. marginal cost of pollution
19. unfunded mandate
20. marginal cost
21. optimum amount of pollution
22. external cost
23. emission charge

TRUE OR FALSE: (HINT)

1. False
2. True
3. True
4. False
5. False
6. True

PEOPLE WHO MATTER: (HINT)

1. John Muir (1838-1914) was an influential American conservationist who helped establish Yosemite and Sequoia National Parks. He also persuaded President Theodore Roosevelt to establish national monuments, national forests, and national parks. The Sierra Club was founded by Muir. Muir Woods National Monument in California was named in his honor.

2. *President Theodore Roosevelt (1858-1919), America's 26th president, sought to conserve the nation's natural resources from private exploitation. Although Congress often opposed him, Roosevelt repeatedly used executive action to add millions of acres of forests and mineral lands to national preserves.*

3. *Read your local paper. Attend a meeting of the planning commission. Contact your local elected officials.*

MAKING CONNECTIONS: (HINT)

1. *Organic waste in the water supply is a form of water pollution. It can enrich the water supply, increasing the biological oxygen demand and killing organisms that require oxygen. (Chapter 21).*

Solid waste disposal in sanitary landfills has a number of problems. It takes up space in sanitary landfills that require large areas. Rain can cause the leaching of chemicals into the water supply. (Chapter 23).

MAKING DECISIONS: (HINT)

1. *Start with table 7.1 in your book. Specific laws will be determined by the physical location and region of the country. The Coastal Zone Management Act might be useful if you live in Florida, but not if you live in New Mexico. Others such as the Water Pollution Control Act, Noise Control Act, and the Endangered Species Act would be worth pursuing anywhere. You can use the following website as a start to gain more information about a specific piece of legislation.*

http://www.cnie.org/nle/crs_titl.shtml#c1

DOING SCIENCE: (HINT)

1. *Hypothesis. If tomato plants are watered with widget waste, they will grow faster. Select tomato seeds that are all of the same variety. Plant them in the same size pots with the same light. Water them the same amount at the same time. Divide up the plants so that some receive plain water (control), some get the fertilizer that is currently used, and others get increasing amounts of widget water. Measure the plant growth of all plants regularly.*

2. *This is a tough problem because the best experiment may not be the best for the environment. Ideally, you'd like to water the field with widget water and then monitor the local water supplies for evidence of the organic material. However, widget water could get into the groundwater and cause a problem. You'd have an answer, but the process would not be environmentally sound. Another problem that could arise would be an argument over where the organic waste in the water actually comes from. There could be a chicken farm nearby that could also be a source of organic waste. You would have to identify some mechanism for tracing the organic waste from your nonpoint source field. You could try doing experiments with tomatoes in pots. Water them at a rate that is approximately equal to the percolation rate of your field and see what amount of organic material leaches out of the pots. You'd expect this to be a high estimate (higher than would occur in a field.*

CHAPTER 8 -- UNDERSTANDING POPULATION GROWTH

LEARNING THE LANGUAGE:

age structure
biotic potential
birth rate (b)
carrying capacity (K)
death rate (d)
density-dependent factor
density -independent factor
developed countries
developing countries
doubling time
evolution
exponential growth
highly developed countries
immigration
industrial stage
K-selection

moderately developed countries
population ecology
population growth momentum
postindustrial stage
preindustrial stage
r -selection
replacement-level fertility
reproductive strategies
survivorship
total fertility rate
transitional stage
type I survivorship
type II survivorship
type III survivorship
zero population growth

CHECKING WHAT YOU KNOW:

MULTIPLE CHOICE:

1. Which of the following is NOT an example of a density-dependent factor?

   A. a lion eating gazelles.
   B. trees competing for sunlight.

   C. a forest fire.
   D. bubonic plague.

2. These factors regulate the size of a population but are not influenced by changes in population density.

   A. rate limiting
   B. density-independent

   C. density-dependent
   D. death

3. The zebra mussels that have invaded the Great Lakes are an example of an r-strategist..
   Which of the following is NOT a characteristic of an r strategist.

   A. many offspring
   B.   short lifespan

   C. nurture offspring
   D. sexually mature at a young age

4. Many endangered species are large animals, that take a long time to mature and produce very few young. They take care of their young until they are old enough to survive on their own. These are examples of

A r strategists

C. survivorship curves

B. K strategists

D. exponential growth

5. Which of the following graphs represents the survivorship curve of an r strategist?

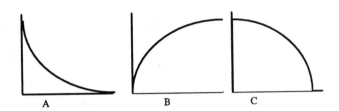

6. Which of the following graphs represents the survivorship curve of a K strategist?

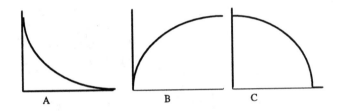

7. The following graph represents

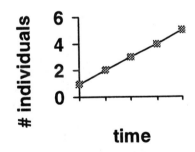

A. carrying capacity

C. linear growth

B. survivorship of an r strategist

D. exponential growth

8. A population increases by

   A. death and immigration.   C. death and emigration.
   B. birth and immigration.   D. birth and emigration.

9. Two factors that decrease the size of a population are

   A. death and emigration   C. immigration and emigration
   B. birth and immigration   D. birth and death

10. The _____ is the number of individuals the total resources of the habitat can support on a sustained basis.

   A. optimum   C. carrying capacity
   B. resource load   D. tolerance limit

11. Which of the following is NOT a characteristic of an organism with Type I survivorship?

   A. Long lifespan   C. Few offspring
   B. Small size   D. Nurture offspring

12. Which of the following is an example of a highly developed country?

   A. Bolivia   C. Uzbekistan
   B. France   D. Laos

13. The transitional demographic stage is characterized by

   A. lower death rates.   C. declining birth rates.
   B. high death rates.   D. high infant death.

14. Which of the following diagrams represents a population that is growing?

   A   B   C

15. An endangered or threatened species, such as a wolf, is most likely to have which kind of survivorship curve?

   A. Type I   B. Type II   C. Type III

16. A(n) _____ is the number and proportion of people at each age in a population.

   A. demographic range
   B. survivorship curve

   C. K selection graph
   D. age structure diagram

17. What is the proper sequence of demographic stages?

   A. preindustrial, industrial, transitional, postindustrial
   B. postindustrial, industrial, transitional, preindustrial
   C. preindustrial, transitional, industrial, postindustrial
   D. industrial, transitional, preindustrial, postindustrial

18. Use the following diagram to determine how many men are between the ages of 5-9 in Nigeria.

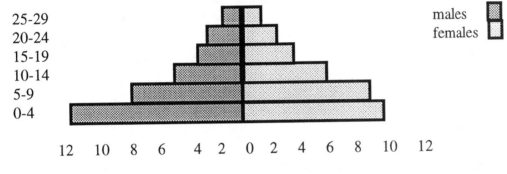

A. 4 million   B. 6 million   C. 8 million   D. 10 million

19. The best definition of population density is:

   A. The number of individual of all species per unit of area of volume.
   B. The number of individuals of one species per unit of area or volume.
   C. The number of individuals of all species per unit of are or volume at a given time.
   D. The number of individuals of one species per unit of are or volume at a
      given time.

20. The growth rate of a population is expressed as:
   A. b—d
   B.
   C. r - td
   D. K - r

FILL IN:

1. _____ _____ deals with the number of individuals of a particular species that are
   found in an area and how and why those numbers change or remain fixed over time.

2. It is projected that the birth rate of humans will equal the death rate toward the end of the 21st century, thus achieving _____ _____ _____.

3. In order to predict the future growth of a population, it is important to know its _____ _____, which is the number and proportion of people at each age in the population.

4. The average number of children born to each woman during her lifetime is the _____ _____ _____.

5. When bacteria divide every 30 minutes, their numbers increase _____.

6. The number of males and number of females at each age, from birth to death, can be represented in a(n) _____ _____ diagram.

7. _____ _____ is the number of individuals of a species per unit of area or volume at a given time.

8. For humans, the _____ _____ is usually expressed as the number of births per 1,000 people per year.

9. GNP stands for _____ _____ _____, the total value of a nation's annual output in goods and services.

10. The maximum rate at which a population could increase under ideal conditions is known as its _____ potential.

11. Because Mexico's birth rate is currently much greater than its _____ _____, it has a high growth rate.

12. The effect of _____ _____ factors on population growth increases as the population density increases.

13. Any environmental factor that affects the size of a population but is not influenced by changes in population density is called a(n) _____ _____ factor.

14. _____ _____ _____ is the number of children a couple must have to "replace" themselves.

15. Humans have been able to provide more _____ and better nutrition by increasing the productivity of agriculturally important crops and animals through selective breeding.

16. Populations _____ in size as long as the birth rate is greater than the death rate.

17. The condition when a population is no longer increasing because the birth rate equals the death rate is called _____ _____ _____.

18. Organisms cannot reproduce indefinitely at their biotic potentials, because the environment sets limits, which are collectively called _____ _____ .

19. There are two types of migration: _____, by which individuals enter a population and thus increase the size of the population, and _____, by which individuals leave a population and thus decrease its size.

20. The rate of change, or growth rate (r), of a population is the birth rate (b) minus the _____ .

21. _____ _____ is the number of years it will take a population to double in size, given its current growth rate.

22. Highly developed countries also have very low _____ _____ _____ s (the number of infant deaths per 1,000 live births).

23. Growth rate is also referred to as _____ _____ in human populations.

24. In populations described by the concept of K̲ selection, _____ has selected traits that maximize the chance of surviving in an environment where population size is near the carrying capacity (K̲) of the environment.

25. Currently, human population is increasing exponentially, although the _____ _____ has declined slightly over the past several years.

TRUE OR FALSE:

1. True   False   A hurricane that causes wind damage to trees is a density-independent factor affecting the population of trees.

2. True   False   In Type III survivorship, the probability of survivorship increases with age.

3. True   False   The carrying capacity represents the largest population that can ever be found in an area.

4. True   False   It is possible for a bacterium that divides every 20 minutes to continue to divide indefinitely.

5. True   False   Population density deals with how and why the number of individuals found in an area remain fixed or change over time.

6. True   False   Birth rate and death rate are two factors to consider when determining the growth rate of a population.

7. True   False   The age structure of a population greatly influences its future population changes.

8. True   False   Pollution, extinction of species, degradation and loss of natural resources, and depletion of energy reserves in today's world are all related to human population growth.

PEOPLE WHO MATTER:

1. Thomas Malthus. Who was Thomas Malthus? What did he do that was significant? Draw a graph that illustrates the point Malthus made.

MAKING CONNECTIONS:

How do limiting factors affect the carrying capacity?

MAKING DECISIONS:

People who believe that Malthus was correct are called Malthusians. There is another group of people called Anti-Malthusians. The Anti-Malthusians believe that technological advances will always make it possible for the food supply to keep up with the population size. One example they cite is the Pleiostene Overkill. The hunter-gatherer societies in what is now Europe so severely depleted the supply of game animals in the region that the size of the human population started to be affected. At this same time, humans learned to cultivate plants and started the domestication of animals. The population recovered and has been increasing ever since.

1. Can you find other examples in your textbook that support the Anti-Malthusians?
2. What evidence can you find that supports the Malthusians?
3. What do you think?

DOING SCIENCE:

1. Ecologists from the University of California at Davis designed an experiment to test the difference between density-dependent and density-independent factors that affect the size of the population of spiders. At the end of their two year study, they decided that a

combination of two density-dependent factors were responsible for determining the population size of the spiders, predation by lizards and competition between lizards and spiders for food. How would you design an experiment to see if predation of spiders by lizards, or competition between lizards and spiders is most significant in determining the size of the spider population?

CHECKING WHAT YOU KNOW: (HINT)

MULTIPLE CHOICE: (HINT)

1. C	*11. B*
2. B	*12. B*
3. C	*13. A*
4. B	*14. B*
5. A	*15. A*
6. C	*16. D*
7. C	*17. C*
8. B	*18. C*
9. A	*19. D*
10. C	*20. A*

FILL IN: (HINT)

1. Population ecology	*14. Replacement-level fertility*
2. zero population growth	*15. food*
3. age structure	*16. increase*
4. total fertility rate	*17. zero population growth*
5. exponentially	*18. environmental resistance*
6. age structure	*19. immigration, emigration*
7. Population density	*20. death rate*
8. birth rate	*21. Doubling time*
9. gross national product	*22. infant death rate*
10. biotic	*23. natural increase*
11. death rate	*24. evolution*
12. density-dependent	*25. growth rate*
13. density-independent	

TRUE OR FALSE: (HINT)

1. True	*3. False*	*5. False*	*7. True*
2. True	*4. False*	*6. True*	*8. True*

PEOPLE WHO MATTER: (HINT)

Malthus was a British economist. He thought that populations would grow exponentially while resources to support populations grow arithmetically. In the following graph, the squares represent population and the diamonds are resources.

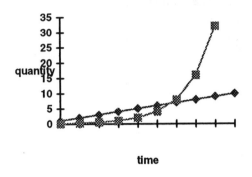

MAKING CONNECTIONS: (HINT)

1. Limiting factors are directly related to a population's carrying capacity. There is some factor in least supply that limits the size of the population even if all other factors are optimal (Chapter 4).

MAKING DECISIONS: (HINT)

1. Look for discussions of food supply and how to increase it. Ways to produce more food and preserve what is available. See Fig. 18-2 on page 404.

2. Look for examples of famine and hunger. See pages 402 to 404.

3. Your informed opinion.

DOING SCIENCE: (HINT)

1. Think about ways to minimize the competition between the lizards and spiders. Use of special cages where the prey can get through but the lizards and spiders cannot? Think about providing plenty of food and then increasing the number of spiders and/or lizards.

CHAPTER 9 -- FACING THE PROBLEMS OF OVERPOPULATION

LEARNING THE LANGUAGE:

birth rate
compact development
consumption overpopulation
contraceptive
death rate
developed country
empowerment of women
family planning
famine
infant mortality rate
migration
mortality

natural resources
nonrenewable resources
overpopulation
people overpopulation
population
pronatalists
renewable resources
reproductive health
resource consumption
total fertility rate
urbanization

CHECKING WHAT YOU KNOW:

MULTIPLE CHOICE:

1. A single child in _____ can cause more environmental harm than 12 children born in Kenya.

    A. China
    B. the United States

    C. India
    D. Bangladesh

2. If a society is to persist, high infant mortality rates must be compensated by

    A. high death rates.
    B. low fertility rates.

    C. increased use of contraceptives.
    D. high fertility rates.

3. Which of the following is NOT a reasonable possibility for a population after the carrying capacity has been reached?

    A. Continued growth at the same rate.
    B. Stabilization of the population
    C. Population crash due to decreased birth rate.
    D. Population crash due to increased death rate.

4. Which of the following is NOT associated with an increase in the fertility rate?

   A. economic development
   B. lack of family planning servcices

   C. lack of education
   D. early marriage

5. Which of the following birth control methods cannot be controlled by the female partner alone?

   A. Diaphragm
   B. Birth Control Pills

   C. Depo-provera
   D. Condom

6. In _____ women are forced to rely on abortion as the primary method of birth control because the cost of contraceptives are prohibitive.

   A. Russia   B. China   C. Japan   D. Germany

7. Which of the following birth control methods prevents sperm from reaching the egg?

   A. Oral contraceptives
   B. Depo-provera

   C. Norplant
   D. Diaphragm

8. _____ the rate of population growth will make nonrenewable resources last longer.

   A. Speeding up   B. Maintaining   C. Slowing

9. Developing nations have _____ overpopulation, in which an increasing number of individuals consume a small share of the resources per person.

   A. people
   B. economic

   C. environmental
   D. consumption

10. Countries with the greatest food shortages have _____ fertility rates.

   A. the lowest   B. equal   C. the highest

11. Which of the following birth control methods does NOT prevent the sperm from entering the uterine tubes?

   A. condom   B. diaphragm   C. birth control   D. vasectomy

12. Developed nations have _____ overpopulation, in which each individual consumes a large share of resources.

   A. people
   B. economic

   C. environmental
   D. consumption

13. The decrease in fertility in most of the countries studied is associated with

   A. increased infant mortality.
   B. low social & economic status of women.

   C. increased use of contraceptives.
   D. decreased use of contraceptives.

14. Which of the following is NOT a factor in the model of the effect of population on the environment?

   A. number of people
   B. resource use per person
   C. environmental damage caused by resource consumption
   D. number of species

15. _____ resources are present in a limited supply.

   A. Renewable
   B. Man-made

   C. Natural
   D. Nonrenewable

16. Which of the following was NOT specifically addressed at the third U.N. International Conference on Population Development in 1994?

   A. Reproductive rights
   B. Empowerment of women
   C. Reproductive health
   D. Increasing lifespan

17. Which of the following policies has NOT been implemented in China?

   A. Mandatory sterilization
   B. Incentives to promote late marriages
   C. Incentives to have only one child per couple
   D. Education and publicity programs

FILL IN:

1. _____ use is strongly linked to lower fertility rates.

2. The motivations for having lots of babies vary from culture to culture, but overall a major reason for high fertility rates is that infant and child _____ rates are high.

3. The economic growth of developing countries is often tied to the exploitation of _____ _____ .

4. _____ resources are present in a limited supply and cannot be replenished in a reasonable period on the human time scale.

5. Several factors affect how quickly nonrenewable resources are used-- including how efficiently the resource is extracted and processed, and how _____ _____, which is how much of it is required or consumed by different groups of people.

6. _____ resources include trees in forests; fishes in lakes, rivers, and the ocean; fertile agricultural soil; and fresh water in lakes and rivers.

7. Those who favor population growth are called _____ .

8. During the 1970s and early 1980s, use of contraceptives in east Asia and many areas of Latin America increased significantly, and these regions experienced a corresponding decline in _____ _____ .

9. In order for a society to endure, it must continue to produce enough children who survive to reproductive age; thus, if infant and child _____ rates are high, fertility rates must also be high to compensate.

10. The increasing convergence of a population in cities is known as _____.

11. _____ _____ includes access to affordable contraception, modern obstetrical practices, and improved maternal and child health care, as well as control of sexually transmitted diseases.

12. _____ _____ is concerned with improving women's status through education and economic opportunities; it is thought that such empowerment will give women more choices and therefore greater control over their reproductive rights.

13. In areas where contraceptive use remains, low there is little or no decline in _____ _____ .

14. _____ _____ occurs when the environment is worsening from too many people, even if those people consume few resources per person.

15. Minerals such as aluminum, tin, and copper, and fossil fuels such as coal, oil, and natural gas, are examples of _____ _____.

16. In _____ _____, cities are designed so that housing is close to shopping and jobs, all of which are connected by public transportation.

17. Mexico is largely _____ compared to other developing countries, although its urban-based industrial economy has not been able to absorb the great number of people in the work force, and unemployment is very high.

18. A country is _____ if the level of demand on its resource base results in damage to the environment.

19. _____ _____ occurs when each individual in a population consumes too large a share of resources.

20. Developing countries have _____ _____, in which the population increase degrades the environment even though each individual uses few resources.

21. _____ _____ have consumption overpopulation, in which each individual in a stable population consumes a large share of resources and the result is environmental degradation.

22. Population education encourages later marriages and birth spacing, both of which reduce the _____ _____ _____.

23. Earth has a finite supply of _____ _____ _____ that sooner or later will be exhausted.

24. _____ _____ _____ is influenced by cultural traditions, women's social and economic status, and family planning.

25. Rapid _____ , together with overpopulation, poverty, and lack of economic development, has caused severe problems in many cities of developing nations.

26. _____ in Europe think that the vitality of their region is at risk because of declining birth rates and that the decrease in population might result in a loss of economic growth.

27. _____, the movement of people from one place to another, is not a solution for overpopulation.

TRUE OR FALSE:

1. True   False   In order for a society to endure, it must continue to produce enough children who survive to reproductive age.

2. True   False   Compulsory sterilization was a failure in India; it had little effect on the birth rate and was exceedingly unpopular.

3. True   False   Urbanization appears to be a factor increasing population growth.

4. True   False   In Japan, oral contraceptives (birth control pills) are illegal, in part because it is feared that their widespread use will further lower the fertility rate.

5. True   False   In areas where contraceptive use is high, there is little or no decline in birth rate.

6. True   False   Family planning forces people to limit their family sizes.

7. True   False   Contraceptive use is strongly linked to lower fertility rates.

8. True   False   Increasing the death rate is an acceptable means of regulating population size.

9. True   False   Contraceptive use promotes small families.

10. True   False   The economic growth of developing countries is often tied to the exploitation of natural resources.

MAKING CONNECTIONS:

1. What is the definition of birth rate and death rate?

MAKING DECISIONS:

1. There are three factors that affect the amount of environmental damage caused by a population: number of people, amount of resources consumed, damage caused by resource consumption. Which of these do you think is the easiest to control?

DOING SCIENCE:

Use the World Population Data sheet inside the back cover of the textbook to answer the following questions.

1. What is the total fertility rate of Botswana?

2. Which country has the highest rate of maternal deaths?

3. Which country has the shortest doubling time?

4. What is the infant mortality rate in more developed countries? In less developed countries?

5. Which continent has the most maternal deaths?

6. Which city has the highest population density?

CHECKING WHAT YOU KNOW: (HINT)

MULTIPLE CHOICE: (HINT)

1. B	6. A	11. C	16. D
2. D	7. D	12. D	17. A
3. A	8. A̶C̶	13. C	
4. A	9. A	14. D	
5. D	10. C	15. D	

FILL IN: (HINT)

1. *Contraceptive*
2. *mortality*
3. *natural resources*
4. ~~*food*~~
4 5. *Nonrenewable*
5 6. *resource consumption*
6 7. *Renewable*
7 8. *pronatalists*
8 9. *birth rate (or fertility rate)*
9 10. *mortality*
10 11. *urbanization*
11 12. *Reproductive health*

13 14. birth rate (or fertility rate)
14 15. People overpopulation
15 16. nonrenewable resources
16 17. compact development
17 18. urbanized
18 19. overpopulated
19 20. Consumption overpopulation
20 21. people overpopulation
21 22. Developed countries
22 23. total fertility rate
23 24. nonrenewable resources
24 25. Total fertility rate
25 26. urbanization
26 27. Pronatalists
27 28. Migration

TRUE OR FALSE: (HINT)

1. true
2. true
3. false
4. true
5. false
6. false
7. true
8. false
9. true
10. true

MAKING CONNECTIONS: (HINT)

1. Birth rate and death rate are expressed as the number of births and the number of deaths per 1000 people per year (respectively).

MAKING DECISIONS: (HINT)

1. You will have to:
- Decide which factor is causing the most environmental problems in the region you are considering.
- Examine the region's moral, ethical, and religious beliefs about family planning.
- Examine the amount and type of environmental damage and the reasons behind it.
- Examine patterns of consumption.

Once you understand what is causing the most harm, you can try to decide if it will be easier to get people to reduce the number of children they are having, change their consumption patterns, or find more environmentally sound ways to consume.

DOING SCIENCE: (HINT)

1. 4.6
2. Sierra Leone
3. Gaza
4. 9; 64
5. Africa
6. Macao

CHAPTER 10 -- FOSSIL FUELS

LEARNING THE LANGUAGE:

acid
acid deposition
acid precipitation
air pollution
anthracite coal
anticline
atmosphere
bituminous coal
black lung disease
calorie
coal
coal gasification
cogeneration
combustion
crude oil
energy
energy conservation
energy efficiency
evaporation
evaporite deposit
fluidized-bed combustion
focus
forest decline

fossil fuel
gas hydrates
hydrocarbons
lignite
lime scrubbers
methane
mineral
natural gas
oil
oil shales
particulate matter
permafrost
petrochemicals
petroleum
scrubbers
SMRCA
strip mining
structural traps
subsurface mining
surface mining
synfuel
tar sand

CHECKING WHAT YOU KNOW:

MULTIPLE CHOICE:

1. Which of the following does not tend to move upward through porous rock layers and accumulate in pools beneath nonporous or impermeable rock layers?

   A. Oil
   B. Natural gas

   C. Tar sands
   D. Crude oil

2. Developed nations consume _____ energy per person than developing nations.

   A. less

   B. the same amount as

   C. more

3. Which of the following is NOT a synfuel?

A. oil shales
B. gas hydrates

C. crude oil
D. coal gas

4. Which of the following is true of surface mining as compared to subsurface mining?

A. It is more expensive.
B. It causes more environmental harm.
C. It allows less coal to be removed.
D. It is generally more dangerous for the miners.

5. Which of the following is NOT a problem likely caused by the combustion of gasoline?

A. Landfill overflow
B. Acid deposition

C. Photochemical smog
D. Global warming

6. Which of the following is NOT part of the Clinton energy strategy?

A. Allow states to set their own speed limits.
B. Increase the efficiency of energy use.
C. Develop a balanced domestic energy resource portfolio.
D. Reinvent environmental protection.

7. Which type of coal is high in sulfur and produces a lot of heat?

A. Anthracite   B. Lignite   C. Bituminous

8. Methane and small amounts of ethane, propane, and butane are the hydrocarbons found in

A. natural gas.
B. petroleum.

C. coal.
D. tar sands.

9. Magnesium sulfate produced in _____ may be used in the dyeing and tanning industries.

A. coal mines
B. photochemical smog

C. scrubbers
D. coal gasification

10. Beginning in the 1940s, oil and natural gas became increasingly important as a fuel because

    A. they can be used to generate electricity, which coal cannot.
    B. wood was less readily available.
    C. natural gas tanks became a status symbol in rural communities.
    D. they are easier to transport and cleaner burning than coal.

11. The pH of normal rain is usually around _____.

    A. 3   B. 5   C. 7   D. 10

12. Which of the following is NOT a method of reducing dependence on fossil fuels from foreign sources?

    A. weatherproofing homes   C. developing energy-efficient products
    B. carpooling   D. eating fat-free potato chips

13. Which of the following fossil fuels is found in the greatest quantities?

    A. Coal   B. Oil   C. Natural gas

14. _____ has acidified lakes and streams, where it has caused aquatic animal populations to decline.

    A. Coal gas   C. Global warming
    B. Photochemical smog   D. Acid deposition

15. _____ is separated into a variety of products during refining.

    A. Coal   C. Crude oil
    B. Natural gas   D. Gasoline

16. Forest decline as a result of air pollution was first documented in _____.

    A. the United States   C. England
    B. Germany   D. Costa Rica

17. Which of the following is NOT a grade of coal

    A. Anthracite
    B. Magnetite
    C. Lignite
    D. Bituminous

18. Which of the following countries has the highest per-capita commercial energy consumption?
    A. United States
    B. Mexico
    C. Egypt
    D. India

19. Which continent has the lowest proved reserves of coal?

    A. Asia
    B. North America
    C. Europe
    D. South America

20. Which area has the largest oil deposits?

    A. North America
    B. Persian Gulf countries
    C. Africa
    D. South America

21. The largest natural gas deposits occur in which country?

    A. Iran
    B. Russia
    C. United States
    D. Saudi Arabia

22. The world's most massive oil spill occurred in 1991 in:

    A. Alaska
    B. the Persian Gulf
    C. the Arctic National Wildlife Refuge
    D. the Russian tundra

FILL IN:

1. _____ mixes crushed coal with particles of limestone in a strong air current during combustion to remove pollutants from the emissions.

2. Farmers in developing nations rely on their own _____ or the energy of animals to plow and tend fields.

3. Propane and butane, separated from natural gas, are stored in pressurized tanks as a liquid called _____ , and used primarily as fuel for heating and cooking in rural areas.

4. Burning soft coals that contain sulfur contributes to _____ .

5. Natural gas that is associated with ice readily dissolves in _____ , which can then be pumped out of the ground.

6. The highest grade of coal is _____ or hard coal. It was exposed to extremely high temperatures during its formation.

7. Many of the conveniences of modern living depend on a ready supply of _____ .

8. _____ is a condition in which the lungs are coated with inhaled coal dust so that the exchange of oxygen between the lungs and the blood is severely restricted.

9. _____ are underground sand deposits permeated with thick, heavy tar or oil heavy that does not move through them.

10. Petroleum, or _____ , is a liquid composed of hundreds of hydrocarbon compounds.

11. If a coal bed is within 30 meters (100 feet) or so of the surface, surface mining (also called open pit mining and _____) is usually done.

12. Oil and natural gas deposits occur in association with _____ such as anticlines and salt domes.

13. Because the concentration of CO_2 in the _____ is increasing and CO_2 prevents heat from escaping from the planet (it acts like glass in a greenhouse), global temperature may be affected.

14. The burning of fuels is called _____ .

15. The _____ requires coal companies to restore areas that have been surface mined, beginning in 1977.

16. Oil contains _____ , compounds that are used in the production of such diverse products as fertilizers, plastics, paints, pesticides, medicines, and synthetic fibers.

17. A(n) _____ is an upward folding of rock strata (layers).

18. The type of air pollution where acid falls from the atmosphere to the surface as precipitation or as dry acid particles is called _____ _____.

19. BTU stands for British thermal unit, an energy unit equivalent to 252 _____.

20. _____ , or crude oil, is a liquid composed of hundreds of hydrocarbon compounds.

21. Fossil fuels are _____ _____; that is, the earth has a finite, or limited, supply of them.

22. Both sulfur oxides and the nitrogen oxides NO and NO_2 form _____ when they react with water.

23. _____ _____ _____ mixes crushed coal with particles of limestone in a strong air current during combustion.

24. The plants selected for revegetation are usually native to the area and thus adapted to the _____ .

25. _____ _____ are reserves of ice-encrusted natural gas deep underground in porous rock.

26. Under a thin upper layer of arctic soil is the _____ layer, which contains permanently frozen water.

27. The most common type of coal is _____. It is also called soft coal even though it is harder than lignite.

28. _____ is a soft coal, brown or brown-black in color, with a soft, woody texture.

29. Production of the combustible gas methane from coal is called _____ _____.

30. Natural gas can be removed from hydrate deposits by pumping _____ (an alcohol) into the hydrate region.

31. _____ _____ develop when extensive salt deposits form at the Earth's surface due to the evaporation of water.

32. _____ are molecules containing carbon and hydrogen that combine to form oil.

33. In _____ _____ , a chemical spray of water and lime neutralizes acidic gases such as sulfur dioxide, which remain behind as a sulfur-containing sludge.

34. In contrast to petroleum, _____ _____ contains only a few different hydrocarbons: methane and smaller amounts of ethane, propane, and butane.

35. Although it is relatively easy to identify and measure pollutants in the _____, it is difficult to trace their exact origins.

36. Oil, natural gas, and coal are _____ _____ that formed several hundred million years ago from plant and animal remains.

37. _____ (collective term for tar sands, oil shales, gas hydrates, liquid coal, and coal gas) are liquid or gaseous fuels that substitute for oil or natural gas.

38. The use of natural gas is _____, in which natural gas is to produce two useful forms of energy, electricity and heat for water and space heating, is known as _____.

39. In order to yield their oil, sedimentary rocks, called _____ _____, must be crushed, heated, and refined after they are mined.

40. If the Great Salt Lake were to dry up, a massive salt deposit called a(n) _____ _____ would remain.

TRUE OR FALSE:

1. True   False   An increase in energy use reduces a country's dependence on costly fuel imports and lessens the harmful environmental impacts of fuel production and consumption.

2. True   False   Natural gas is the cleanest of the fossil fuels.

3. True   False   Subsidies increase the cost of fuel for consumers, whereas energy taxes decrease the cost.

4. True   False   The goal of a national energy strategy should be to ensure adequate energy supplies without harming the environment.

5. True   False   From the 1600s through the 1800s, wood was the predominant fuel in the United States.

6. True   False   Natural gas produces harmful particulate matter the way coal and oil fuels do.

7. True   False   Hydrocarbons produce photochemical smog.

8. True   False   Prior to passage of the 1977 Surface Mining Control and Reclamation Act (SMCRA), abandoned surface mines were usually left as large open pits.

MAKING CONNECTIONS:

1. There are many things that can be done to improve the efficiency of machines, factories and processes that use fossil fuels. Explain why even a phenomenal improvement (say 1000%) isn't the final answer to meeting our energy needs.

2. Organisms on the tundra grow very slowly. This ecosystem is very slow in its ability to rid itself of pollutants. Why is this true?

MAKING DECISIONS:

1. Make a list of things that will reduce dependence on fossil fuels. How many of the things on your list can you do personally today? Identify those items on your list that require future research and development. Are there things on this list that you can contribute to, given your career plans?

2. Compare and contrast the views of those who support development of the Arctic National Wildlife Refuge and those who oppose oil exploration in this region. Which side do you agree with? What can you do to make your opinion be heard?

3. Senator Byrd of West Virginia has been a key opponent of clean air legislation in the United States Senate. He does not do this because he is against environmental issues nor does he do this because he favors dirty air. What is Senator Byrd's justification for his position?

CHECKING WHAT YOU KNOW: (HINT)

MULTIPLE CHOICE: (HINT)

1. C
2. C
3. C
4. B
5. A
6. A
7. C
8. A
9. C
10. D
11. B
12. D
13. A
14. D
15. C
16. B
17. B
18. A
19. D
20. B
21. B
22. B

FILL IN: (HINT)

1. Fluidized-bed combustion
2. physical energy (or energy)
3. liquefied petroleum gas
4. acid deposition
5. methanol
6. anthracite
7. energy
8. black lung disease
9. Tar sands
10. crude oil
11. strip mining
12. structural traps
13. atmosphere
14. combustion
15. SMCRA
16. petrochemicals
17. anticline
18. acid deposition
19. calories
20. petroleum
21. nonrenewable resources
22. acids
23. Fluidized-bed combustion
24. climate
25. gas hydrates
26. permafrost
27. bituminous coal
28. Lignite
29. coal gasification
30. methanol
31. salt domes
32. hydrocarbons
33. lime scrubbers
34. natural gas
35. atmosphere
36. fossil fuels
37. Synfuels
38. cogeneration
39. oil shales
40. evaporite deposit

TRUE OR FALSE: (HINT)

1. False	3. False	5. True	7. True
2. True	4. True	6. False	8. True

MAKING CONNECTIONS: (HINT)

1. No matter how efficient our energy consumption is, we will still be depleting fossil fuels. These are nonrenewable resources. This means that they cannot be regenerated at a rate that is useful on a human time scale. We need to find other alternatives to fossil fuels that are renewable.

2. The tundra grows slowly because of the low energy input to the climate. Look up the climate in your book (chapter 5). The climate is also responsible for the inability to process or dilute pollutants. Think about how the cold temperatures and slow growth will affect these processes.

MAKING DECISIONS: (HINT)

1. Several possibilities: walk or ride a bike, car pool, or use public transportation; purchase items that use less packaging; develop and use manufacturing processes that use alternatives to fossil fuels or extract the most out of the fuel that is burned.

2.

Supporters	Opposition
infrastructure exists	existing infrastructure will probably have to be expanded
improve balance of trade	create greater dependence on foreign oil
19% probability oil exists is enough	100% probability is not high enough to warrant environmental damage
little impact on environment	lasting negative impact
damage that does occur isn't worth restoration	damage that does occur isn't worth restoration
economic development	spend money on alternate fuels
jobs	

Decide which side you support. Find all the facts you can. Write letters to key individuals such as Congress members. Write letters to editors. Draft an Op/Ed piece and submit it to your local paper. Check out the Internet for information sources and groups that share your beliefs.

3. Most of the bituminous coal in the United States is found in Appalachia, particularly West Virginia. This type of coal has high amounts of sulfur and is used to fuel power plants in the Midwest. The Midwest has been accused of causing the acid rain that is

damaging ecosystems in the Northeastern United States. Clean air legislation tends to reduce the use of bituminous coal, which reduces coal mining in West Virginia. Severe economic harm is caused to the region when high sulfur coal use becomes restricted. Senator Byrd fights this legislation to keep jobs in his state.

CHAPTER 11 -- NUCLEAR ENERGY

LEARNING THE LANGUAGE:

atom
atomic mass
atomic number
breeder reactor
chain reaction
combustion
containment building
control
control rod
cooling tower
decommission
deuterium
disease
DNA
electrons
energy
enrichment
entombment
fission
fossil fuel
fuel rods
fusion

half-life
high-level radioactive wastes
ionizing radiation
isotope
low-level radioactive waste
matter
meltdown
mutations
neutrons
nuclear energy
nuclear reactor
oncogenes
radiation
radioactive
radioisotope
reactor vessel
steam generator
tritium
turbine
uranium-235
vitrification

CHECKING WHAT YOU KNOW:

MULTIPLE CHOICE:

1. Which of the following is NOT a viable option when a nuclear power plant has reached the end of its usable life?

    A. decommission
    B. conversion to coal

    C. entombment
    D. storage

2. The biggest environmental problem associated with nuclear power is

    A. radioactive air pollution.
    B. risk of DNA damage caused by human exposure during normal operations.
    C. ground water contamination from the core.
    D. long term storage of radioactive wastes.

3. A(n) _____ is an atom that has a different number of neutrons than another atom with the same atomic number. .

    A. isotope   C. neutron
    B. ion   D. electron

4. The _____ water circuit cools the condenser which cools the spent steam in the power plant.

    A. primary   C. tertiary
    B. secondary   D. quartenary

5. _____ have mass, a positive charge, and are found in the nucleus.

    A. Electrons   B. Neutrons   C. Protons   D. Ions

6. What is the atomic number of the following element?

```
+----------+
|    10    |
|    Ne    |
|  20.18   |
+----------+
```

    A. 10   B. 20   C. 20.18   D. 30.18

7. The half-life of radon-226 is 1600 years. If you start with 1 kg at noon, how much will you have at 5 p.m.?

    A. 0 kg   B. 0.25 kg   C. 0.5 kg   D. 1 kg

8. Which of the following is the only radioactive isotope of hydrogen?

    A. Deuterium   C. Tritium
    B. Uranium-238   D. Plutonium

9. Which of the following is NOT located in the containment building?

    A. reactor vessel   C. fuel rods
    B. steam generator   D. cooling tower

10. Radioactive particles cause damage to DNA molecules by

    A. destroying repair enzymes.
    B. entering the lungs.
    C. causing cancer.
    D. breaking the DNA strands.

11. Damage to DNA in the _____ is most likely to have lasting consequences in later generations.

    A. brain or eyes
    B. gastrointestinal tract
    C. bone marrow
    D. ovaries or testes

12. Nuclear waste from nuclear power plants is a matter of international security risk because

    A. radioactive waste cannot be contained by international boundaries.
    B. the Yucca mountain waste disposal site lies near a fault line.
    C. meltdowns in developing nations are common and extremely dangerous.
    D. plutonium can be converted to use in nuclear weapons.

13. Which of the following elements is used to produce additional P-239 in a Breeder reactor?

    A. Radon -226
    B. Tritium
    C. Strontium - 90
    D. Uranium - 238

14. What does NIMBY stand for?
    A. no interest in medicinal biology yet
    B. no interest in metallic byproducts of yucca mountain
    C. nuclear industry may become yucca mountain
    D. not in my back yard

15. Which of the following is NOT a component of an atom

    A. ion
    B. electron
    C. neutron
    D. proton

16. Which of the following fuels are commonly used in fission?

    A. Uranium-235
    B. Tritium
    C. Strontium - 90
    D. Radon - 226

17. Which type of power plant generates more fuel?

    A. nuclear reactor   C. fission reactor
    B. breeder reactor   D. coal-fired reactor

18. Which of the following is a concern about fusion?

    A. It generates large amounts of radioactive wastes.
    B. No one knows if the reaction can be regulated at the extremely high temperatures
       required.
    C. It produces weapons grade radioactive wastes
    D. Fuel is hard to find and expensive to process.

19. The half-life of iodine is approximately 2.5 hours. If you start with 1 kg of iodine at noon,
    how much will you have left at 5 p.m.?

    A. 0 kg   B. 0.25 kg   C. 0.5 kg   D. 1 kg

20. A single uranium dioxide pellet containing 3% U-235 contains the energy equivalent of

    _____.

    A. three coal-fired power plants   C. one ton of coal
    B. 6 gallons of gasoline   D. 5,000 gallons of seawater

21. The following diagram illustrates how electricity is produced. Which of the following
    sources can be used to turn the turbine with the least amount of environmental damage?

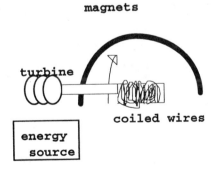

    A. coal.   B.   nuclear fuel.   C.   human   D.   water.

22. Carbon rods in the reactor core of a nuclear power plant

    A. slow chain reactions by absorbing particles that trigger the splitting of atoms.
    B. are the radioactive fuel source.
    C. cause a chain reaction by splitting into radioactive isotopes that heat water.
    D. cool the reactor by recycling water from the environment.

23. Most radiation to which humans are exposed comes from

    A. radon.
    B. medical x-rays.

    C. nuclear fuel.
    D. outer space.

24. What is the biggest advantage to fusion should it become a commercially viable process for the generation of electricity?

    A. The fuel, hydrogen, is abundant.
    B. Has less air pollution.
    C. Generates more energy per molecule.
    D. Research is going on in Germany, Japan, and Russia.

25. The accident at Chernobyl:

    A. was second only to Three Mile Island in environmental damage.
    B. spread radiation unevenly over certain areas of Europe and Asia.
    C. has been followed by 3 other explosions of unsafe reactors in Ukraine.
    D. was immediately followed by large numbers of breast cancer, stomach cancer, and other organ cancers in survivors.

26. Yucca Mountain is a possible storage site for

    A. commercially-produced high-level nuclear wastes.
    B. commercially-produced low-level nuclear wastes.
    C. military-produced low-level nuclear wastes.
    D. military-produced liquid nuclear wastes.

FILL IN:

1. The amount of time required for one-half of a radioactive substance to change into a different element is called the _____ _____.

2. The energy released in combustion and other chemical reactions comes from changes in the _____ _____ that hold the atoms together.

3. The number of _____ in each atom of a given element may vary, resulting in atoms of one element with different atomic masses.

4. Excess heat from a nuclear fission reaction is controlled by pumping hot water from the condenser to a massive _____ _____.

5. Ore is refined to increase the content of U-235 from 0.71% to 3% in a process called _____.

6. Elements are considered to be _____ if they spontaneously emit a form of energy called radiation.

7. The _____ is turned by the steam produced in the steam generator and produces electricity.

8. When the _____ of an atom of U-235 is struck by and absorbs a neutron, it becomes unstable and splits into two smaller atoms, each approximately half the size of the original uranium atom.

9. When radiation is emitted from a radioactive isotope, the nucleus changes into a different element. This process is called _____ _____.

10. _____ _____ contains enough energy to eject electrons from atoms, which results in the formation of positively-charged atoms called ions.

11. In breeder nuclear reactors, both U-235 and Pu-239 are split to release _____.

12. In _____, two smaller atoms are combined to make one larger atom of a different element.

13. The _____ _____ is where the heat produced by nuclear fission is used to produce steam from liquid water.

14. _____ _____ involves the nucleus of an atom.

15. Unstable isotopes are called _____.

16. _____ provides a blueprint for all characteristics of an organism and directs the activities of cells; damage to it is almost always harmful to the organism.

17. _____ are radioactive solids, liquids, or gases that initially give off large amounts of ionizing radiation.

18. Uranium 235 (U-235 or 235U) is an isotope of uranium with a(n) _____ _____ of 235.

19. _____ contains one proton and two neutrons per nucleus.

20. Nuclear energy involves changes within the nuclei of _____ ; small amounts of matter from the nucleus are converted into very large amounts of energy.

21. _____ contain a nucleus made of positively-charged particles (protons) and particles with no charge (neutrons).

22. The splitting of an atomic nucleus into two smaller fragments, accompanied by the release of a large amount of energy is called _____.

23. Both fission and fusion result in a significant release of energy in comparison to the chemical combustion of _____ _____.

24. When _____ occur in reproductive cells (that is, eggs or sperm), the changes can be passed on to the next generation, where they might result in birth defects, mental retardation, or genetic disease.

25. _____ _____ is the energy released by nuclear fission or fusion.

26. _____ is where the entire power plant is permanently encased in concrete which must remain intact for at least one thousand years.

27. Solidifying liquid waste into solid glass logs, is known as _____

28. The _____ of an element is equal to the sum of protons and neutrons in the nucleus.

29. The number of protons is equal to the _____ _____ of the element.

30. In a nuclear power plant, the reactor core where fission occurs is surrounded by a huge steel potlike structure called a _____ _____. This prevents the release of radioactivity into the environment.

31. A human-made hydrogen isotope, formed during the fusion reaction by bombarding another element, lithium, with neutrons, is called _____. It is weakly radioactive and not found in nature.

32. _____ contains one proton and one neutron per nucleus.

33. _____ _____ keep positively-charged protons together in the nucleus.

34. By exactly controlling the placement of the _____ _____, the plant operator can produce the exact amount of fission required.

35. In _____ _____ _____, U-238 is converted to plutonium, Pu-239, a human-made isotope that is fissionable.

36. At high temperatures the metal encasing the uranium fuel can melt, releasing radiation; this is called a(n) _____.

37. Mutations in normal genes involved in the control of growth and development may convert them to _____, which are cancer-causing genes.

38. Exposure of individuals to very high levels of _____ may cause such severe physiological damage that death can occur.

39. _____ _____ absorb neutrons in reactor cores, forming radioisotopes.

40. Uranium-235 has an atomic mass of 235 and a(n) _____ _____ of 92.

41. _____ are radioactive solids, liquids, or gases that give off small amounts of ionizing radiation.

TRUE OR FALSE:

1. True False In comparison to fossil fuels, nuclear energy emits very few pollutants into the atmosphere.

2. True False Nuclear reactions produce 100,000 times less energy per atom than do chemical reactions such as combustion.

3. True False Although conventional nuclear power plants cannot explode like atomic bombs, accidents can happen in which dangerous levels of radiation might be released into the environment and result in human casualties.

4. True False Nuclear energy has less of an environmental impact than fossil fuels.

5. True False One of the most dangerous effects of ionizing radiation is the damage it does to DNA, the genetic material of organisms.

6. True False Nuclear power plants can operate for only 250 years before certain critical sections, such as the reactor vessel, become brittle or corroded.

7. True   False   Fusion is the type of nuclear reaction that is currently being used in power plants world wide.

8. True   False   An uncontrolled nuclear fission reaction takes place when nuclear weapons explode.

9. True   False   Radioisotopes with short half-lives are still considered a problem because they mimic essential elements in the body.

10. True   False   Human error contributed to the Chernobyl disaster.

11. True   False   The steam coming out of cooling towers contains radioactive fallout.

12. True   False   People living near coal-fired power plants are exposed to more radioactive emissions than people living near nuclear power plants.

MAKING CONNECTIONS:

1. Why is nuclear energy generated from fission considered a nonrenewable resource?

2. In what ways does nuclear energy contribute to environmental problems associated with atmospheric pollution?

MAKING DECISIONS:

1. There are many processes that use radioactive isotopes other than nuclear power plants. Many medical procedures use radioisotopes as does medical research. These procedures generate radioactive waste that must be disposed. Somewhere in your town or in a nearby town is a storage facility that is holding these waste materials until they can be placed in long-term storage. Keep in mind, these local storage facilities do NOT contain weapons grade plutonium or waste from nuclear power plants. This is small amounts of radiation used for things like medical treatments.

Currently there are many discussions of how to permanently store such wastes and where those storage facilities should be located. List some issues that are associated with making these decisions. What do you think?

2 After studying nuclear power and fossil fuels, list the advantages and disadvantages to each as a fuel source. Which do you think holds the most promise for meeting the energy needs of the future?

DOING SCIENCE:

1. One of the few examples of acute human exposure to high levels of radiation occurred at Hiroshima and Nagasaki. The victims of these bomb blasts have been studied extensively, and research shows that there may be some genetic damage to successive generations. However, the results are not statistically significant. What does this mean? How should this information be used when considering the implications of other accidental exposures? What are the ethical questions that should be considered?

2. In the 1940s and 1950s many experiments were done to examine the effect of radiation on humans. Often, the subjects of the experiments were not told of the nature of the experiment or of the potential risk. In other cases, volunteers willingly participated in the experiments and are proud of their participation today. Why were these experiments allowed to occur during this time period?

CHECKING WHAT YOU KNOW: (HINT)

MULTIPLE CHOICE: (HINT)

1. B	8. C	15. A	22. A
2. D	9. D	16. A	23. A
3. A	10. D	17. B	24. B
4. C	11. D	18. B	25. A
5. C	12. D	19. B	
6. A	13. D	20. C	
7. D	14. D	21. C	

FILL IN: (HINT)

1. half-life
2. chemical bonds
3. neutrons
4. cooling tower
5. enrichment
6. radioactive
7. turbine
8. nucleus
9. radioactive decay
10. ionizing radiation
11. energy
12. fusion
13. steam generator
14. nuclear power
15. radioisotopes
16. DNA
17. High-level radioactive wastes
18. atomic mass
19. tritium
20. Atoms
21. fission
22. fossil fuels
23. mutations
24. Nuclear energy
25. Entombment
26. vitrification
27. atomic mass
28. atomic number
29. reactor vessel
30. tritium
31. Deuterium
32. atomic forces
33. control rods
34. breeder nuclear fission
35. meltdown
36. oncogenes
37. radiation
38. Fuel rods
39. atomic number
40. Low-level radioactive wastes

TRUE OR FALSE: (HINT)

1. True	4. True	7. False	10. True
2. False	5. True	8. True	11. False
3. True	6. False	9. True	12. False

MAKING CONNECTIONS: (HINT)

1. It is nonrenewable because, just like fossil fuels, there is a finite amount of radioactive isotopes on the planet. While the supply may last for thousands of years, it will still get used up eventually.

2. The process of enrichment requires energy. This energy is currently in the form of fossil fuels that emit air pollutants. Mining can contribute particles to the atmosphere and also uses energy. Small amounts of radioactive gas can be released from reactors.

MAKING DECISIONS: (HINT)

1. To be safe, the storage site must be long-term.
Radioactive material can't leak into groundwater.
Radioactive dust can't escape into the atmosphere.
Materials that could be used for nuclear weapons should not be accessible to individuals who wish to make such instruments.

Risk assessment should be performed when choosing between a single site like Yucca Mountain, with its 1000 year risk of earthquake, and the consequences of current short-term storage. Is it better to keep low levels of radiation in towns and neighborhoods where it is currently stored, or is better to bring it together in one site where it gets concentrated?

2.

Coal-fired	Nuclear fission
mining/drilling required	*mining/drilling required*
nonrenewable	*nonrenewable*
hazardous to workers	*hazardous to workers*
air pollution	*little air pollution*
Produces CO_2 -- greenhouse gas	*no greenhouse gas*
	long-term waste storage problems
no radiation exposure	*potential radiation exposure*

DOING SCIENCE: (HINT)

1. The fact that the results are not statistically significant means that while there is genetic damage in the population, it is not statistically different (greater or less) than the amount of genetic damage found in populations not exposed to the fallout from the atomic bomb blasts. Therefore it cannot be said conclusively that the type of exposure suffered here caused the genetic damage. It could be from conditions that already existed. This makes it difficult to make broad statements about the risks of genetic damage (associated with acute exposure to radiation from an atomic bomb). The ethical considerations are mostly related to future generations. What should a pregnant woman do if she is exposed to radiation? Will the fetus be damaged as a result? Should men and women of childbearing age who are exposed to radiation be encouraged to NOT have children because the risk of damage to their gametes could affect potential offspring? A second ethical consideration is the genetic damage that leads to cancers. Will an individual approach life differently under the threat of getting a cancer later in life?

2. During this time period, we did not know anything at all about radiation. We knew that it was a powerful force. TNT is also a powerful force, and there were no known health effects from carrying it around. People volunteered because they felt they were contributing to the body of knowledge and participating in research at the frontier of science. Informed consent laws did not exist at this time.

Search the internet for sites that relate to these experiments.

CHAPTER 12 -- RENEWABLE ENERGY AND CONSERVATION

LEARNING THE LANGUAGE:

active solar heating
alcohol fuels
alternative energy sources
biogas digestor
biomass
cogeneration
deforestation
desalinization
electricity
energy
energy conservation
energy efficiency
energy intensity
geothermal energy
hydrologic cycle
hydropower
indirect solar energy
infrared radiation
kinetic energy

latitude
National Appliance Energy
 Conservation Act
ocean temperature gradients
ocean thermal energy conversion
passive solar heating
photovoltaic cells
potential energy
radiation
renewable energy resource
resource recovery
schistosomiasis
solar energy
solar pond
solar thermal electric generation
sun
tidal energy
turbine
wind farms

CHECKING WHAT YOU KNOW:

MULTIPLE CHOICE:

1. _____ is a clean fuel that produces only water and heat when it burns.

    A. Sulfur   B. Uranium   C. Hydrogen   D. Oxygen

2. Intensive use of _____ for energy has resulted in deforestation and desertification, soil erosion, air pollution, and degradation of water supplies.

    A. oil   B. wood   C. biomass   D. sunlight

3. Which of the following is an example of direct solar energy?

    A. Running a car on electricity generated from a photovoltaic cell.
    B. Running a car on ethanol produced from corn.
    C. Using a sail to wind surf.
    D. Running a car on a new fuel made of 50% water.

4. The _____ set efficiency standards for household appliances.

   A. Environmental Protection Agency
   B. National Appliance Energy Conservation Act
   C. Energy Policy Act
   D. National Environmental Policy Act

5. Many renewable energy sources are inefficient because

   A. they don't exist in great quantities.
   B. they must be collected or concentrated to be useful.
   C. they must be dispersed to be useful.
   D. they are hard to find and collect.

6. Which source of energy involves hot rocks and steam?

   A. wind power
   B. hydropower
   C. geothermal energy
   D. radiant energy

7. When energy is converted from one form to another, some useful energy is lost usually in the form of heat. This is the

   A. law of tolerance
   B. competitive exclusion principle
   C. first law of thermodynamics
   D. second law of thermodynamics

8. When _____ is burned to produce energy, some of the pollution problems caused by fossil fuel combustion are not present.

   A. uranium
   B. biomass
   C. a solar cell
   D. energy

9. Which of the following is an example of improved energy efficiency?

   A. carpooling
   B. riding a bicycle to work
   C. driving slower
   D. buying a car with better mileage

10. Which of the following fuels is NOT likely to be depleted if used wisely?

    A. oil
    B. coal

    C. wood
    D. natural gas

11. Which of the following can NOT be done with solar energy?

    A. convert cold water to warm water
    B. make a car go.

    C. generate electricity
    D. convert Uranium to electricity

12. In which of the following regions/applications is solar energy most cost effective?

    A. Heating homes in Northwest Ohio.
    B. Heating water in Alaska.

    C. Pumping water in London.
    D. Refrigerating vaccines in Nigeria.

13. Which of the following is an example of increased energy efficiency?

    A. Burning coal for heat.
    B. Replacing coal with biomass to generate electricity.
    C. Drilling for oil in unendangered habitats.
    D. Cogeneration of heat and electricity.

14. Energy conservation is

    A. moderating or eliminating wasteful energy-consuming activities.
    B. using technology to do things with less energy.
    C. using energy for essential functions only.
    D. using technology to generate more energy.

15. Which of the following are NOT positively affected by an increase in energy conservation and efficiency?

    A. environmental damage from chloroflourocarbons
    B. environmental damage from air pollution
    C. environmental damage from acid precipitation
    D. environmental damage from coal mining

16. Which of the following countries is NOT significantly increasing its use of geothermal energy?

    A. England
    B. Japan

    C. Nicaragua
    D. United States

17. Which appliance uses the most electricity in a year?

    A. a 75 watt light bulb
    B. a microwave oven

    C. a hot water heater
    D. a refrigerator

18. A city's total commercial energy consumption divided by its gross domestic product give its

    A. energy conservation
    B. energy rating

    C. energy efficiency
    D. energy intensity

19. Relative to combustion of bituminous coal, low levels of _____ are produced when biomass is burned.

    A. carbon dioxide and nitrogen oxides
    B. nitrogen and carbon

    C. sulfur and ash
    D. oxygen and carbon dioxide

20. The production of energy from ocean temperature gradients is called

    A. solar energy conversion.
    B. tidal energy.

    C. ocean thermal energy conversion.
    D. wave power.

21. Which of the following does NOT affect the intensity of solar radiation?

    A. latitude
    B. longitude

    C. season of the year
    D. time of day

22. Which of the following sources of energy is NOT concentrated in highly localized areas?

    A. sunlight   B. coal   C. uranium   D. oil

23. It is unlikely that photovoltaic cells will be used for large-scale production of electricity because

    A. they operate by collecting energy from the sun.
    B. they are more efficient than lead batteries
    C. they can only be used on space craft like the MIR where the solar energy is greatest.
    D. they require too much space.

24. Which state would have the greatest probability of success in implementing direct solar technologies?

    A. Maine   B. Wisconsin   C. Arizona   D. Idaho

25. Which of the following is NOT a consequence of improving energy conservation and efficiency?

    A. reduced photosynthetic production   C. reduced acid precipitation
    B. reduced air pollution   D. reduced dependence on fossil fuels

FILL IN:

1. One type of _____ is crop residues, which includes cornstalks, wheat stalks, and wood wastes at paper mills and sawmills.

2. People in areas such as Africa, Central America, India, and China, where fragile ecosystems are continually being destroyed by _____, are already beginning to use solar box cookers because wood for fuel is in short supply.

3. The removal of salt from water is called _____.

4. _____ is a tropical disease, caused by a parasitic worm, that can damage the liver, urinary tract, nervous system, and lungs.

5. _____ is surface air currents that are caused by the solar warming of air.

6. In _____ _____ _____, a series of collection devices mounted on a roof or in a field is used to gather solar energy.

7. Biomass can be converted to liquid fuels such as methanol and ethanol. These are also called _____ _____.

8. _____ is considered an example of indirect solar energy because it is the result of photosynthesis.

9. A country's or region's total energy consumption divided by its gross domestic product gives its _____ _____.

10. _____ is the production of two forms of energy (usually, electricity and useful heat) from the same fuel.

11. A controlled flow of water released down the spillway of a dam turns a _____, which generates electricity.

12. The traditional way to produce _____ is to use some type of fuel to provide heat to form steam from water.

13. _____ _____ _____ are becoming increasingly important, both because they are renewable and because their use generally has less environmental impact than the use of fossil fuels or nuclear power.

14. The potential energy of water held back by a dam is converted to _____ _____ as the water falls down a penstock, where it turns turbines to generate electricity.

15. Lower _____ are closer to the equator and receive more solar radiation annually than do those closer to the north and south poles.

16. In _____ _____ _____, solar energy is used to heat buildings without the need for pumps or fans to distribute the collected heat.

17. In _____ , after the steam is used to generate electricity, it supplies energy to heat buildings, cook food, or operate machinery before it is cooled and pumped back to the boiler as water.

18. _____ is organic material that is used as a source of energy.

19. Electricity can be produced by several different systems that employ _____, in which concentrated sunlight produces high temperatures in a fluid.

20. Arrays of non-polluting wind turbines called _____ _____, have sprung up in many open landscapes, the rotors of each turbine spinning furiously to generate electricity when the wind blows.

21. To increase _____ _____, technology is designed to accomplish a particular task with less energy.

22. The _____ _____ encompasses evaporation from land and water, transpiration from plants, precipitation, and drainage and runoff.

23. _____ _____ is more intense when the sun is high in the sky than when it is low in the sky.

24. A pond of water designed specifically to collect solar energy is called a(n) _____ _____.

25. _____ use microbial decomposition of household and agricultural wastes to produce biogas that is used for heating and cooking.

26. _____ _____, which convert solar energy directly into electricity, they are wafers or thin films of crystalline silicon that are treated with certain metals in such a way that they generate a flow of electrons when solar energy is absorbed.

27. _____ offers a convenient way to store solar energy as chemical energy.

28. The _____ sets national appliance efficiency standards for refrigerators, freezers, washing machines, clothes dryers, dishwashers, air conditioners, and water heaters.

29. In a solar collector, _____ _____ cannot penetrate glass, heat does not escape, and the interior grows continuously warmer.

30. _____ _____ _____ can be used to heat water, heat buildings, and generate electricity.

31. Biomass, wind, and hydropower are all examples of _____ _____. _____.

32. The energy of flowing water, or _____, exists because of the hydrologic cycle that is driven by solar energy.

33. The _____ produces a tremendous amount of energy, most of which dissipates into outer space and a very small portion of which is radiated to the Earth.

TRUE OR FALSE:

1. True   False   It is possible to offset the CO_2 that is released into the atmosphere from biomass combustion by increasing tree planting.

2. True   False   Energy consumption is our single most important long-term energy solution.

3. True   False   The most promising alternative energy technologies use solar energy.

4. True   False   The combustion of biomass is an example of direct solar energy.

5. True   False   The United States has a greater energy intensity than Japan or Germany.

6. True   False   Solar hydrogen is produced by sunlight in outer space.

7. True   False   Demand-side management helps consumers save energy.

8. True   False   Infrared radiation is given off as visible light.

9. True   False   Solar thermal energy systems are currently more efficient at trapping direct sunlight than other solar technologies.

10. True   False   Houses heated with solar technology can be built without any backup system.

MAKING CONNECTIONS:

1. Explain how the sun drives hydrologic cycle.

2. Review what you know about the energy pyramids and food webs (pp 51-56 in the text). What classification of organisms is most responsible for biomass accumulation? What process is involved? How does this process relate to the past accumulation of fossil fuels?

MAKING DECISIONS:

1. What can you do to reduce your own energy consumption?

DOING SCIENCE:

1. There are certain desert plants that are loaded with organic molecules similar to common petroleum-based fuels. What do you need to know about these plants before you can determine their usefulness as renewable fuel sources?

2. The following table gives the amount of hydrocarbons produced per gram dry weight (plant material) for four different species. Based on these data, which of these species would be the best to use as a renewable resource?

Species	Hydrocarbons/gram dry weight
A	67
B	3563
C	794
D	1708

3. The following table gives some details about the growth requirements of each species. The type of soil preferred is either sand or sand with some organic material. Sand is easy to obtain. The nutrients are Nitrogen (N), Potassium (K), and Phosphorus (P), with a small requirement for Manganese by species B. The rainfall for the regions in which these plants grow is also given.

Species	Soil	Nutrients	rainfall requirements
A	Sand	N,P,K	1/2 " month year round
B	Sand with some humus	N,P,K,Mn	1" month year round
C	Sandy with humus	N,P,K	Seasonal rains with long dry spells
D	Sand	N,P,K	Seasonal rains with long dry spells

Given this information, which species seems to be best for development as a renewable fuel source? Why?

CHECKING WHAT YOU KNOW: (HINT)

MULTIPLE CHOICE: (HINT)

1. C	6. C	11. D	16. A	21. B
2. B	7. D	12. D	17. D	22. A
3. A	8. B	13. D	18. D	23. D
4. B	9. D	14. A	19. C	24. C
5. B	10. C	15. A	20. C	25. A

FILL IN: (HINT)

1. biomass
2. deforestation
3. desalinization
4. Schistosomiasis
5. Wind
6. active solar heating
7. alcohol fuels
8. Biomass
9. energy intensity
10. Cogeneration
11. turbine
12. electricity
13. Alternative energy sources
14. kinetic energy
15. latitudes
16. passive solar heating
17. cogeneration
18. Biomass
19. solar thermal electric generation
20. wind farms
21. energy efficiency
22. hydrologic cycle
23. Solar radiation
24. solar pond
25. Biogas digestors
26. Photovoltaic cells
27. Hydrogen
28. National Appliance Energy Conservation Act
29. infrared radiation
30. Direct solar energy
31. indirect solar energy
32. hydropower
33. sun

TRUE OR FALSE: (HINT)

1. True
2. False
3. True
4. False
5. True
6. False
7. True
8. False
9. True
10. False

MAKING CONNECTIONS: (HINT)

1. First review (pp 87- 88 in the text) and diagram the hydrologic cycle. The sun provides the energy that causes evaporation and transpiration. It is also responsible for the air currents that move the cloud masses that deposit rain.

2. Producers, or autotrophs, cause the accumulation of biomass. The further away from producers, the more energy that is lost through energy conversions, so the burning of plant biomass would convert more solar energy than the burning of animal waste and decomposition materials.

The process that allows plants to accumulate biomass is photosynthesis.

Photosynthesis is directly related to the production of fossil fuels because fossil fuels were made from the remains of plants and animals.

MAKING DECISIONS: (HINT)

1. Make a list of things that you can do, such as taking shorter showers and using more efficient lightbulbs. When you are considering various alternatives, make a list of the evidence supporting each one (the benefits, the costs). Remember that you must make decisions based on the best science possible and what fits with your own belief system.

DRIVE TO SCHOOL	WALK TO SCHOOL	RIDE BIKE TO SCHOOL
takes the least amount of time	takes a long time	longer than in car, but better than walking
uses gasoline	uses my energy	uses my energy
does not improve health	improved health	improved health
what is the accident risk	what is the accident risk?	what is the accident risk?
Car gets stolen		bike gets stolen?
requires car $$$	requires shoes $	requires bike $$
find parking space		find parking space
can carry lots of books and materials	can carry few books and materials	can carry few books and materials

DOING SCIENCE: (HINT)

1. Observe the plant in its native habitat. What does it need to survive? How does it fit in the food chain? What are the limiting factors to growth? What other organisms are located there?

Bring samples into your lab and determine how much fuel they can actually produce.

2. Species B produces the most hydrocarbons per gram dry weight. Since it seems to be most productive, it is likely candidate for further study.

3. While specie B produces the most hydrocarbons, it also has the most stringent growing requirements. It needs a nutrient that is not found in the standard mixes. It will take energy and cause environmental damage to produce that nutrient. It also has the greatest water requirements. Species D only produces half of the amount of hydrocarbons, but its growing conditions are less restrictive. It is likely that it will be more efficient to use D as the renewable energy source particularly in developing nations or desert regions without ready access to fresh water and fertilizers.

CHECKING WHAT YOU KNOW: (HINT)

MULTIPLE CHOICE: (HINT)

1. A	7. A	13. D	19. C
2. A	8. C	14. D	20. B
3. A	9. D	15. C	21. C
4. C	10. B	16. B	
5. C	11. B	17. D	
6. C	12. D	18. C	

FILL IN: (HINT)

1. vaporized
2. Irrigation
3. runoff
4. stable runoff
5. hydrogen bond
6. desalinization
7. hydrologic cycle
8. drainage basin
9. aquifers
10. Surface water
11. reverse osmosis
12. Distillation
13. evaporation
14. confined aquifer
15. reservoirs
16. aquifer depletion
17. flood plains
18. deserts
19. semiarid lands
20. salinization
21. climate
22. Reservoirs
23. flood control
24. groundwater
25. microirrigation
26. recycling
27. flood irrigation
28. flood plains
29. Wetlands
30. water table
31. transpiration
32. groundwater
33. Subsidence
34. saltwater intrusion
35. delta or estuary

TRUE OR FALSE: (HINT)

1. true
2. true
3. false
4. true
5. false

PEOPLE WHO MATTER: (HINT)

1. Powell was exploring the canyon for scientific purposes and to expose the potential for human exploitation. He was also an adventurer. Secretary Babbitt is interested in restoring the ecology of the canyon that has been damaged by the Glenn Canyon Dam and by human traffic through the region. This was also a scientific experiment to observe

the impact of releasing flood waters into the canyon. The site where three of Powell's fellow travelers left his party and were killed by Indians is now buried under Lake Meade. You can imagine the conversation between the two men where Secretary Babbit is asking what was it like and Powell is asking how has it changed.

MAKING CONNECTIONS: (HINT)

1. Review the discussion in chapter 6 on spring and fall turnover. Remember that turnover allows the water to mix, bringing nutrients up from the sediments and oxygenating the lower regions of the lake. As freshwater is withdrawn from a lake, its salinity increases, and affects the density of water. Because turnover is caused by changes in the density of water as the temperature of the water changes, increased salinity may hamper or enhance turnover. Shallower water may also affect turnover. (Very shallow water does not exhibit thermal stratification.)

MAKING DECISIONS: (HINT)

1. Use the Colorado River, the Aral Sea, and Lake Mono as potential examples.

PRO	CON
Could be good as a mechanism to control floods?	*Increase in salinity?*
Reduce population in region?	*Depletion of available water?*
Use flow to generate electricity?	*Loss of habitat?*
Use as control threat over southwest?	*Loss of wetlands adjacent to the lakes?*
	Reduce population in region?

How will you advise your member of Congress?

DOING SCIENCE: (HINT)

1. Hypothesis I: Implementation of conservation strategies will increase the supply of water. Measure levels of local rivers or reservoirs before implementation and compare them to after implementation.
Hypothesis II: Implementation of conservation strategies will reduce the amount of waste water generated. Measure the rate of water treatment before and after implementation.

CHAPTER 14 -- SOILS AND THEIR PRESERVATION

LEARNING THE LANGUAGE:

A-horizon
B-horizon
bacteria
C-horizon
castings
clay
compost
conservation tillage
contour plowing
conventional tillage
crop rotation
dust bowl
E-horizon
food
humus
illuviation
leaching
loam
mineral depletion

mineral nutrients
mollisols
mulch
mycorrhizae
O-horizon
runoff
shelterbelt
soil
soil erosion
soil horizons
soil profile
spodosol
strip cropping
terracing
terrestrial
topography
weathering processes
wind

CHECKING WHAT YOU KNOW:

MULTIPLE CHOICE:

1. Examine the map in figure 14-13. Which region of the world has fewer soil problems (some concern or stable)?

    A. Australia
    B. United State

    C. South Africa
    D. Europe

2. The _____ originates from weathering of the underlying bedrock.

    A. A-horizon   B. B-horizon   C. C-horizon   D. E-horizon

3. _____ enable plants to absorb essential minerals from the soil more efficiently.

    A. Roots
    B. Mycelium

    C. Illuviation
    D. Mycorrhizae

4. Which of the following is NOT an inorganic soil particle size?

    A. sand   B. silt   C. loam   D. clay

5. The organic material contained in humus can _____ the ability of soil to hold water.

    A. increase   B. not affect   C. decrease

6. Which of the following is NOT a method of farming that specifically reduces erosion?

    A. desalinization   C. crop rotation
    B. terracing   D. no-tillage

7. Which major soil group is found in the arid regions of all continents?

    A. spodosols   B. aridosols   C. mollisols   D. alfisols

8. Which of the following materials should NOT be added to a compost pile?

    A. Yard waste such as grass clippings
    B. Food scraps such as potato peelings
    C. Materials found in household wastebaskets
    D. Shredded newspapers and sawdust

9. The material that passes through the earthworm's digestive tract is _____.

    A. humus   B. castings   C. soil water   D. mycelium

10. Microorganisms such as bacteria and fungi are most active in decomposing organic material in which soil horizon?

    A. A-horizon   B. B-horizon   C. C-horizon   D. E-horizon

11. Which type of soil has the best aeration?

    A. sandy soil   B. loam   C. clay soil   D. humus

12. Which of the following organisms is most important in aerating soil?

    A. earthworms
    B. plants

    C. fungi
    D. bacteria

13. The dust bowl in the central United States in the 1930s was caused by

    A. water erosion
    B. strip mining

    C. mineral depletion
    D. wind erosion

14. Which of the following is NOT a problem or concern associated with municipal solid waste composting?

    A. Finding a source of materials to compost
    B. Heavy metals contained in sewer sewage sludge
    C. Batteries and household chemical waste
    D. Finding a market for the compost

FILL IN:

1. In _____ _____, fields are plowed and planted in curves that conform to the natural contours of the land, rather than in straight rows.

2. Conserving our soil resources is critical to human survival because more than 99 percent of our _____ comes from the land.

3. Much of the bulky waste in sanitary landfills, including paper, yard refuse, and food wastes, is organic and, given the opportunity, could decompose into _____ .

4. Sand particles are large enough to be seen easily with the eye. Silt particles, which are about the size of flour particles, are barely visible with the eye. _____ particles are too small to be seen with an ordinary light microscope.

5. It may take centuries for abandoned barren land to return to its natural state; until then, it will be susceptible to erosion, especially by _____.

6. _____ _____, the removal of soil from the land by the actions of water, wind, ice, and other agents, is a natural process that is often accelerated by human activities such as deforestation and farming on arid land.

7. The deposit of leached material in the lower layers of soil is known as _____.

8. _____ is partly decomposed organic material in the soil.

9. Beneath the _____ is the topsoil, or A-horizon, which is dark and rich in accumulated humus.

10. The _____ is below the extent of most roots and is often saturated with groundwater.

11. A typical _____ _____ would be corn in year one, soybeans in year two, followed by oats in year three and alfalfa in year four.

12. The _____ _____ that occurred in the western united states during the 1930s is an example of accelerated wind erosion caused by human exploitation of marginal land for agriculture.

13. Beneath the B-horizon is the _____, which contains weathered pieces of rock and borders the unweathered solid parent material.

14. The removal of dissolved materials from the soil by water percolating downward is called _____.

15. Soybeans and alfalfa, both members of the legume family, increase soil fertility through their association with _____ that fix atmospheric nitrogen into the soil.

16. Associations between plants and fungi, called _____, enable plants to absorb adequate amounts of essential minerals from the soil.

17. _____, which makes ideal agricultural soil for most climates, has approximately equal portions of sand, silt, and clay.

18. In a balanced ecosystem, _____ cycle from the soil to organisms and then back again to the soil.

19. The presence or absence of mountains and valleys is part of a region's surface characteristics or _____.

20. Soil is formed from rock by chemical and physical _____ _____ that make smaller and smaller particles.

21. _____ are found in colder climates. They have an acidic litter layer, leached E-horizon, and an illuvial B-horizon.

22. In _____ _____ residues from previous crops are left in the soil, covering it and holding it in place.

23. _____ produces level areas, reducing erosion in mountainous areas.

24. _____ _____ is a special type of contour plowing that produces alternating strips of different cops along natural contours.

25. One of the best ways to reduce the effects of wind on soil erosion is to plant _____.

26. _____ is placed on the surface of soil to control weeds and reduce evaporation.

27. _____ are found in temperate grasslands and are very fertile. They have a thick A-horizon that is rich in humus.

28. The bits of soil that pass through the gut of an earthworm are called _____.

29. The horizontal layers of soil that can be seen by examining a deep vertical section of the ground are called _____ _____.

30. _____ _____ occurs when the minerals in the soil are leached out by irrigation or rainfall.

31. The complex material in which plants take root is called _____.

True or False.

1.　True　False　Although conservation tillage is an effective way of reducing soil erosion, it requires greater use of herbicides to control weeds.

2.　True　False　Soil, which is composed of inorganic minerals, organic materials, soil air, and soil water, is often organized into layers called vistas.

3.　True　False　The pH of most soils ranges from 1 to 4.

4.　True　False　Nimbyism – the not in my backyard syndrome – frequently takes hold when government officials attempt to find new places for sanitary landfills.

5.　True　False　Humans often accelerate soil erosion with poor soil management.

MAKING CONNECTIONS:

1. A routine environmental impact statement being prepared for an industrial development project revealed the presence of a population of rare arthropods living in the soil. This species is not threatened or endangered, so it is not possible to stop development of the site. The managers, however, would like to try avoid negative publicity by relocating the population to a different site. What information do you need to gather about this organism and its soil habitat before you can decide where the most likely relocation site would be?

2. How is human overpopulation related to worldwide soil problems?

MAKING DECISIONS:

1. Go on to the first question under Doing Science. After you finish answering that question, make a list of all the steps you must go through before relocating the species. Be sure to include social and economic considerations.

2. Compare and contrast strip cropping, conservation tilling, crop rotation, contour plowing, and terracing method(s). Which method(s) would be most appropriate where you live?

DOING SCIENCE:

1. Design an experiment to test whether the rare species of arthropod will survive in the new location. How will you keep track of small soil dwelling arthropods? How will you estimate the size of the new population?

2. You are working in forensics. You find a soil sample that contains traces of a toxic substance in the tires of a vehicle. You are trying to determine where the toxin was dumped. The car is linked to the suspects who stole the material. You believe that if you can trace where the soil in the tires comes from, you will be able to pick a likely area to begin the search for this toxic material. Given what you have learned about soil and how it is formed, how would you go about tracing the soil sample to its source?

CHECKING WHAT YOU KNOW: (HINT)

MULTIPLE CHOICE: (HINT)

1. A	5. A	9. B	13. D
2. C	6. A	10. A	14. A
3. D	7. B	11. A	
4. C	8. C	12. A	

FILL IN: (HINT)

1. contour plowing
2. food
3. compost
4. Clay
5. wind
6. Soil erosion
7. illuviation
8. Humus
9. O-horizon
10. C-horizon
11. crop rotation
12. dust bowl
13. C-horizon
14. leaching
15. bacteria
16. mycorrhizae
17. Loam
18. mineral nutrients
19. topography
20. weathering processes
21. Spodosols
22. conservation tillage
23. Terracing
24. Strip cropping
25. shelterbelts
26. Mulch
27. Mollisols
28. castings
29. soil horizons
30. Mineral depletion
31. soil

TRUE OR FALSE: (HINT)

1. true	3. false	5. true
2. false	4. true	

MAKING CONNECTIONS: (HINT)

1. What is the niche of the arthropod? What does it eat? Who eats it? What are the limiting factors (see chapter 4)? To determine limiting factors and micronutrients, you will have to profile the soil. What is the soil type? What is the pH? Particle size? Amount of organic material? Local climate?

2. As population increases the need for food increases. Food production disturbs soil, causes erosion and depletion of minerals. People also must occupy space. Their houses and buildings are being built on productive farmland thereby reducing the amount of available and land and making it harder to produce food. Human wastes also take up space in landfills and contaminate soils.

MAKING DECISIONS: (HINT)

1.
- *Study the organism in its natural habitat.*
- *Identify limiting factors, food web relationships, niche, habitat.*
- *Locate potential sites based on light, water, climate, etc.*
- *Test the soil for pH, moisture, composition, etc., and identify the site that is closest to the original.*
- *Look at the soil profile and soil types.*
- *Experiment by moving a few organisms.*
- *Answer questions about the cost of moving the species versus the cost of moving the site.*
- *How will you deal with the situation if it is not possible to move the arthropods or if the move fails?*

2.

strip cropping	conservation tilling	crop rotation	contour plowing	terracing
can be combined with other plowing methods	can be combined with strip cropping, crop rotation, terracing	can be combined with plowing methods	can be combined with other plowing methods	can be combined with plowing methods
hilly terrain	any terrain	any terrain	hilly terrain	hilly terrain
reduces erosion	reduces erosion	maintains soil fertility	reduces erosion	reduces erosion
can reduce pests and therefore pesticide use	increases herbicide use	reduces pests and therefore pesticide use	no effect on pesticide use	no effect on pesticide use

Look at the terrain where you live. Is it hilly? What is the climate? What types of crops are traditionally grown? Match this information with the benefits and drawbacks of each method.

DOING SCIENCE: (HINT)

1. You may do tests in the laboratory. If site B is appropriate for our arthropod, then organisms in an aquarium containing soil from site B will do as well as organisms in an aquarium containing soil from the original site. Keep everything constant in the environment but the soil. If that works, you may release a limited number of arthropods in the new site and observe them.

You may mark and recapture the organisms. Any unmarked ones you recapture will represent new organisms.

2. You will characterize the material and compare it to soils in the area. Remember that soil is formed from a weathering process where the parent material or rock breaks down into the smaller particles that make up the components of soil. You would examine the soil for these particles to see if the rock they came from provide a clue. You can examine the soil for organic components. Can you identify traces of the organisms that live in it (forest leaves, swamp plants, etc.)? Look for trace minerals to compare. Can you determine the soil horizon? What are the soil particle sizes?

CHAPTER 15 -- MINERAL: A NONRENEWABLE RESOURCE

LEARNING THE LANGUAGE:

acid mine drainage
arid land
bacteria
bioleaching
blast furnace
coke
constructed wetlands
dematerialization
derelict lands
energy
energy conservation
environmental cost
evaporation
food web
General Mining Law of 1872
high-grade ores
hydrothermal processes
hyperaccumulator
industrial ecology
industrial ecosystem
life index of world reserves
low-grade ores
magmatic concentration
manganese nodules
metal
metal sulfides
mineral
mineral conservation
mineral reserves
mineral resource

nometallic minerals
oil
open-pit surface mining
ore
overburden
oxides
pipes
precipitation runoff
recycling
reuse
rocks
sanitary landfills
sedimentation
shaft mine
silt
slag
slope mine
smelting
spoil bank
strip mining
subsurface mining
sulfur
sulfides
surface mining
Surface Mining Control and Reclamation
    Act of 1977
sustainable manufacturing
tailings
total resources
world reserve base

CHECKING WHAT YOU KNOW:

MULTIPLE CHOICE:

1. It is expensive to obtain high quality metal from low-grade ores because

    A. it takes a lot of energy to get enough ore.
    B. high-grade ore is harder to extract.
    C. low-grade ores are only found in remote locations.
    D. it takes very little energy to extract low-grade ores.

2. A mineral resource is

    A. an estimate of the time remaining before the known amounts are used up.
    B. a list of the deposits that are identified and currently profitable.
    C. the rate of consumption.
    D. a list of deposits of low-grade ore of little current profitability.

3. It takes a constructed wetland _____ years to neutralize the acids sufficiently for life to survive in the rivers downstream from acid mine damage.

    A. 5-10   B. 10-50   C. 50-100   D. 100-500

4. Which of the following countries is NOT a developed country that is also in the top five mineral producing nations in the world?

    A. Brazil   C. Canada
    B. United States   D. Australia

5. Traditional industries operate in a linear fashion. Which of the following most closely resembles this pathway?

    A. natural resources ---> products ---> wastes
    B. wastes ---> natural resources ---> products
    C. products --->natural resources ---> wastes
    D. natural resources ---> wastes ---> products

6. Relative to developing countries, developed countries

    A. use most of the mineral resources.
    B. have more of the mineral resources.
    C. have used up less of their mineral resources.
    D. are using fewer of the mineral resources.

7. Sulfur dioxide from open-air smelters reacts with _____ to form sulfuric acid, a component of acid rain.

    A. oxygen   B. nitrogen   C. soil   D. water

8. Which of the following will NOT encourage low waste practices?

   A. Introduction of specific conservation techniques.
   B. Modification of public attitudes about resource conservation.
   C. Reduction of the cost of resources.
   D. Increases in public awareness of resource conservation.

9. Which of the following is NOT a step in converting a mineral deposit into a usable product.

   A. Locate the ore.   C. Refine the ore.
   B. Mine the ore.   D. Recycle the ore.
                                         10.   D. aluminum

10. Which of the following is NOT a reasonable substitute for tin in canmaking and packaging?

   A. lead   B. plastic   C. glass   D. aluminum

11. Which of the following is NOT a plan typical of programs regulating mining operations?

   A. reduce pollution
   B. restore mining sites
   C. provide price supports for mineral development.
   D. protect recreational and wilderness sites from development

12. Which of the following is NOT a common destructive side effect of small-scale gold mining?

   A. soil erosion   C. production of silt
   B. air pollution   D. mercury contamination

13. Which of the following does NOT affect the estimates of mineral reserves?

   A. economics   B. politics   C. technology   D. ecology

14. Examine figure 15-7. What percentage of the world total consumption of copper does the United States consume?

   A. 30 %   B. 24 %   C. 15%   D. 4.6%

15. Manufacturers must _____ if consumers are to be able to decrease their consumption.

   A. make recyclable products
   B. make durable products
   C. make disposable products
   D. make inexpensive products

16. Surface mining disturbs the land _____ subsurface mining.

   A. more than   B.   less than   C.   the same amount as

17. Subsurface mining is better than surface mining because

   A. it is more expensive.   C. it disturbs less land.
   B. it is more hazardous for miners.   D. it extracts minerals.

18. Which of the following is an example of dematerialization?

   A. tailfins on cars   C. string Bikinis
   B. laptop computers   D. lightweight bikes

FILL IN:

1. _____ processes can extract phosphates at room temperature.

2. In _____, used items such as beverage cans and scrap iron are collected, remelted, and reprocessed into new products.

3. _____, a component of sulfuric acid, is an indispensable industrial mineral with many applications in the chemical industry.

4. Acids and other toxic substances in the _____ _____ of mines are washed into soil and water by precipitation runoff.

5. In _____ _____, the wastes produced by one company are sold to another company as raw materials for their processes, in a manner analogous to nutrient recycling in nature.

6. _____ _____ are mineral deposits that have been identified and are currently profitable to extract.

7. The combination of a mineral's reserves and resources is called its total resources or its _____ _____ _____.

8. A mineral's _____ is an estimate of the time it will take for the known reserves of that mineral to be expended.

9. _____ _____ are a way to use natural processes that occur in marshes and ponds to neutralize acid enough for aquatic life to return to rivers and streams downstream from acid mine drainage but, it typically takes 50 to 100 years.

10. One effective way to correct _____ _____ _____ is to construct a series of marshes or ponds downstream from the mine.

11. _____ is modified coal that is used as an industrial fuel in blast furnaces.

12. Reclamation of areas that were surface mined for coal is required by the

_____.

13. Processing minerals often involves _____, which is melting the ore at high temperatures to help separate impurities from molten metal.

14. Historically, the _____ _____ of minerals has not been incorporated into the actual price of mineral products to consumers.

15. _____ _____ are substances that are not good conductors of electricity; they include sand, stone, salt, and phosphates.

16. Weathered particles can be transported by water and deposited as sediment on riverbanks, deltas, and the sea floor in a process called _____.

17. Today's _____ _____ may become tomorrow's mines, as valuable minerals and other materials are extracted from them.

18. Purified copper, tin, lead, iron, manganese, cobalt, or nickel _____ is done in a blast furnace.

19. _____ _____ are deposits of low-grade ores that may or may not be profitable to extract in the future.

20. As products evolve, they tend to become lighter in weight and often smaller. This decrease in the weight of products over time is called _____.

21. The _____ was established to encourage settlement in the sparsely-populated western states.

22. _____ _____, which are extensively damaged due to mining, can be restored to prevent further degradation and to make the land productive for other purposes.

23. Minerals that are too deep to be removed by surface mining are extracted by _____ _____.

24. _____ are mineral compounds in which certain elements are combined chemically with sulfur.

25. Treating low-grade gold ores with _____ such as *Thiobacillus* allows a 90 percent recovery of gold, compared to 75 percent recovery for the more expensive and energy-intensive conventional methods.

26. Significant worldwide deposits of common table salt ($NaCl$), borax ($Na_2B_4O_7$), potassium salts, and gypsum ($CaSO_4\text{-}2H_2O$) have been formed by _____.

27. Limestone reacts with impurities in ore to form a molten mixture called _____.

28. Deposits of _____ _____ _____ are potential sources of minerals that are currently unprofitable to extract but may be profitable to extract in the future.

29. A_____ is a rare plant that absorbs high quantities of a metal and stores it in its cells.

30. _____ _____ includes recycling and reuse.

31. Acids and other toxic substances in the spoil banks of mines are washed into soil and water by _____ _____.

32. _____ are mineral compounds in which elements are combined chemically with oxygen.

33. In an industrial ecosystem, industries are linked to one another in complex ways that resemble a _____ _____ in a natural ecosystem.

34. As molten rock cools it often separates into layers with heavy minerals on the bottom, in a proccess called _____ _____.

35. Because _____ _____ are not soluble in water, they form deposits by settling out of the solution.

36. _____ _____ _____ contain relatively large amounts of particular minerals, whereas low-grade ores contain lesser amounts.

37. Canadian geologists pinpointed the site of a whole cluster of _____, the veins that carry diamonds to the surface from great depths.

38. The combination of a mineral's reserves and resources is called its _____ _____.

39. In _____ _____, a trench is dug to extract the minerals from the ground.

40. _____, loose rocks produced during the mining process, are usually left in giant piles on the ground or in ponds near mineral processing plants.

41. One of the most significant economic factors in mineral production is the cost of _____ .

42. _____ are small rocks the size of potatoes that contain manganese and other minerals, such as copper, cobalt, and nickel, and are found on the ocean floor.

43. During strip mining a new trench is dug parallel to the old one; the overburden from the new trench is put into the old trench, creating a hill of loose rock known as a _____ .

44. Elements and compounds that occur naturally in the Earth's crust are called _____.

45. _____ is the overlying layers of soil and rock that must be removed before minerals can be extracted from a strip mine.

46. _____ _____ involve groundwater that has been heated in the Earth and that carries minerals through cracks and fissures in the rock.

47. A mixture of minerals that has varied chemical concentrations is called _____.

48. Acids and toxic substances found in the spoil banks of mines can leach into nearby streams, rivers, and groundwater causing _____ _____ _____.

49. Bottles and cans that are _____ are collected, washed, and refilled.

50. A company that practices _____ _____ will find ways to convert wastes into useful products.

51. Minerals that are located near the surface of the Earth are extracted by _____ _____.

52. _____ _____ is the study of mechanisms to use resources efficiently and create products out of wastes.

53. _____ is rock that contains sufficient concentrations of a mineral to make mining profitable.

54. In _____, a large hole is dug to gain access to the minerals, usually iron, copper, stone and gravel.

55. A _____ _____ is used to smelt ore.

TRUE OR FALSE:

1. True   False   Plants such as cattails and bulrushes that are planted in the shallow waters of constructed wetlands help to trap acid in the sediments.

2. True   False   Reuse of a glass bottle simply requires washing it, which obviously expends more energy than recycling.

3. True   False   If our mineral supplies are to last and if our standard of living is to remain high, consumers must decrease their consumption.

4. True   False   One effective way to correct acid mine drainage is to construct a series of marshes or ponds downstream from the mine.

5. True   False   Low-grade ores contain fewer pollutants than high-grade ores.

6. True   False   One effective way to cut production costs is to substitute an inexpensive or abundant material for an expensive or scarce one.

7. True   False   In arid regions, the vast amounts of water required during the extraction and processing of minerals may be the limiting factor.

8. True   False   Dredging manganese nodules from the ocean floor would increase biodiversity in the oceans.

9. True   False   Like other natural resources, mineral deposits in the Earth's crust are distributed evenly.

10. True   False   The benefits of reuse are even greater than those of recycling.

11. True   False   Smelting plants have the potential to emit large amounts of air pollutants during mineral processing.

12. True   False   Beverage container laws increase the amount of tax money needed to reduce litter and solid waste.

13. True   False   Surface mining is more common because it is less expensive than subsurface mining.

14. True   False   Although dematerialization gives the appearance of reducing consumption of minerals and other materials, it can sometimes have the opposite effect.

MAKING CONNECTIONS:

1. If you think of the Kalundborg industrial ecosystem as a food web, who are the producers?

2. Explain how erosion from mining affects fish in a river downstream.

3. How does an electrostatic precipitator function?

MAKING DECISIONS:

1. Check your local newspaper, broker, or bank for the price of gold today. Assume that the price of gold has doubled. You know that there are trace amounts of gold in the hills that surround your town. At the current price, the cost of extracting the gold from such low-grade ore becomes attractive. What other costs should be figured into the balance sheet before the real profit from this ore can be realized?

DOING SCIENCE:

1. You have found a few plants growing on the worst part of the Copper Basin. Until now, no reclamation projects have worked here. You think that these plants might be doing well here because they are hyperaccumulators of some mineral left in the damaged soils of the region. How will you determine if these plants are hyperaccumulators?

Ch. 15

CHECKING WHAT YOU KNOW: (HINT)

MULTIPLE CHOICE: (HINT)

1. A	6. A	11. A	16. ~~B~~ A
−2. D	7. D	12. C	17. ~~A~~ C
3. C	8. C	13. B	18. ~~C~~ B
4. A	9. D	14. ~~D~~ B	~~19. B~~
5. A	10. D	15. B	

FILL IN: (HINT)

1. Bioleaching
2. recycling
3. Sulfur
4. spoil banks
5. industrial ecosystems
6. Mineral reserves
7. world reserve base
8. life index of world reserves
9. Constructed wetlands
10. acid mine drainage
11. Coke
12. Surface Mining Control and Reclamation Act of 1977
13. smelting
14. environmental cost
15. Nonmetallic minerals
16. sedimentation
17. sanitary landfills
18. smelting
19. Mineral resources
20. dematerialization
21. General Mining Law of 1872
22. Derelict lands
23. subsurface mining
24. Sulfides
25. bacteria
26. evaporation
27. slag
28. low-grade ores
29. hyperaccumulator
30. Mineral conservation
31. precipitation runoff
32. Oxides
33. food web
34. magmatic concentration
35. metal sulfides
36. High-grade ores
37. pipes
38. total resources
39. strip mining
40. Tailings
41. energy
42. Manganese nodules
43. spoil bank
44. minerals
45. Overburden
46. Hydrothermal processes
47. rock
48. acid mine drainage
49. reused
50. sustainable manufacturing
51. surface mining
52. industrial ecology
53. Ore
54. open-pit surface mining
55. blast furnace

TRUE OR FALSE: (HINT)

1. true	5. false	9. false	13. true
2. false	6. true	10. true	14. true
3. true	7. true	11. true	
4. true	8. false	12. false	

MAKING CONNECTIONS: (HINT)

1. The producers are the organizations that bring the energy from the environment into the community. The power plant and the oil refinery are the producers.

2. Erosion contributes particulate matter, or silt, to the rivers. This silt can clog the waterways. If the eroded material includes toxic chemicals, these can contaminate the water and kill aquatic life. If the erosion includes contaminants like nitrogen or phosphorus, it can cause cultural eutrophication.

3. An electrostatic precipitator gives the particles in an industrial emmission a positive charge so that they will cling to negatively charged plates and not pass out of the smokestack. You can demonstrate an electrostatic precipitator by tearing a few small pieces of paper and holding a comb that you have run through your hair over them. The small pieces of paper will be attracted to the comb.

MAKING DECISIONS: (HINT)

1. You must consider the cost of meeting any environmental regulations that are imposed on a mining effort. Governmental agencies may require remediation plans for disturbed areas and extensive pollution control measures that could be very costly. You should also consider the implications of the type of mining. How much habitat will be destroyed? What is the potential for water pollution? How many species could be lost or displaced? What is the value of altering land that has been used for recreational purposes such as hiking, biking, and nature walks? How can you place a monetary value on these things?

DOING SCIENCE: (HINT)

1. Take some samples of these plants and burn the plants, carefully collecting the ash. Leach the minerals from the ash and use chemical tests to determine the composition of these minerals. Compare these minerals to the soils in the area. Do the same experiment with these plants growing in other regions or soils that are not contaminated. How do the plants' mineral compositions change?

CHAPTER 16 -- PRESERVING EARTH'S BIOLOGICAL DIVERSITY

LEARNING THE LANGUAGE:

adaptive radiation
artificial insemination
atmosphere
background extinction
bacteria
bellwether species
biodiversity
biological diversity
biological diversity treaty
biotic pollution
commercial extinction
commercial harvest
commercial hunting
community
conservation biology
Convention on International Trade in
Endangered Species (CIPES)
culling
deep ecology
deforestation
ecosystem
ecosystem diversity
embryo transfer
endangered species
Endangered Species Act
evolution
exotic species
experimental, nonessential species
ex situ conservation

extinction
flyways
game farming
genetic diversity
genetic engineering
habitat
in situ conservation
island
mass extinction
National Biological Service (NBS)
national conservation strategy
natural product
overpopulation
population density
range
seed banks
species
species diversity
sport hunting
subsistence hunting
succession
threatened
threatened species
UV radiation
wilderness
wildlife management
wildlife ranching
World Conservation Strategy

CHECKING WHAT YOU KNOW:

MULTIPLE CHOICE:

1. Which of the following is NOT a direct cause of the destruction of the ecological balance of Lake Victoria?

    A. Overfishing
    B. Pollution

    C. Ozone depletion
    D. Biotic pollution

2. What is the most significant cause of declining biological diversity?

A. habitat reduction
B. introduction of foreign species

C. pollution
D. pest control

3. Which of the following is NOT a characteristic of a species that is likely to be endangered or go extinct?

A. Each organism produces many offspring.
B. The species has an extremely small range.
C. The size of the total population is very small.
D. There is a low reproductive success for the population.

4. The number of species we consume for food is _____ relative to the total number of edible species.

A. small
B. high

C. equal to
D. in proportion to

5. Which of the following is NOT commercial harvesting?

A. Selling breeding pairs to zoos.
B. Selling research animals to laboratories.
C. Selling parrots to pet shops.
D. Selling furs to the garment industry.

6. _____ try to affect a species by manipulating the plant cover, food, and water supplies of its habitat.

A. Conservation biologists
B. Ecologists

C. Environmentalists
D. Wildlife managers

7. The annual global trade in animals is a multibillion dollar industry. One-third of this is illegal because it:

A. is based on products that support wildlife management.
B. represents an increase in biodiversity.
C. involves rare, threatened, or endangered species.
D. involves predator and prey species for biological control.

8. It is estimated that _____ of every 2000 species that ever existed are extinct today.

   A. 1   B. 99   C. 199   D. 1999

9. Conservation biologists estimate that species are becoming extinct approximately _____ the rate of background extinction.

   A. 10   B. 100   C. 1,000   D. 10,000

10. The formation of an anaerobic zone at the bottom of Lake Victoria is an example of

    A. biotic pollution   C. biodiversity
    B. habitat destruction   D. deep ecology

11. The cichlids in Lake Victoria

    A. were an important source of protein for humans.
    B. cannibalize their young for food.
    C. had a population explosion as a result of abundant food.
    D. were introduced in 1960.

12. Which of the following is NOT true of extinction?

    A. It occurs when the last member of a species dies.
    B. It can be reversed through adaptive radiation.
    C. It is both natural and human caused.
    D. It represents a permanent loss of biodiversity.

13. Deep ecologists believe

    A. that humans should take precedence over animals.
    B. that all organisms have the right to exist.
    C. that Noah's Ark is an example of species conservation.
    D. that all extinctions must be prevented.

14. Which of the following environmental problems does NOT affect remote, undisturbed areas?

A. climate change
B. solid waste

C. ozone depletion
D. acid rain

15. Species of bacteria and fungi are important in biological diversity because

A. they are consumers.
B. they are decomposers.

C. they are producers.
D. they are parasites.

16. Subsistence hunting is NOT a major cause of extinction today because subsistence hunters:

A. only kill what they can eat.
B. sell only what they cannot consume.
C. profit from the organisms they capture.
D. support very few human groups.

17. Which of the following is NOT a benefit of storing seeds in seed banks?

A. A large amount of plant genetic material is stored in a small space.
B. Some species have been re-introduced into natural habitats from seeds.
C. Seeds in seed banks are evolutionarily stagnant.
D. Seeds in seed banks are protected from habitat destruction.

18. Which of the following is NOT an example of ex situ conservation?

A. captive breeding
B. storing seeds

C. artificial insemination
D. establishing a wildlife reserve

19. One environmental benefit to sport hunting is it can:

A. effectively control overpopulation.
B. cause commercial extinction.
C. introduce new species into a region.
D. provide targets for people with guns.

20. Which of the following states has the most serious problem with declining biodiversity?

A. Ohio
B. Oklahoma

C. New Hampshire
D. California

21. The declining numbers of an endangered species represent a decline in biodiversity because their _____ is diminished.

    A. habitat diversity
    B. genetic diversity

    C. species diversity
    D. ecosystem diversity

22. Which of the following is NOT something that must be determined before scientists can re- introduce a species into a natural habitat?

    A. What factors originally caused the species to become extinct in nature.
    B. Whether the factors that caused the original extinction still exist.
    C. Whether any suitable habitat remains.
    D. What conditions are necessary for captive breeding to be successful.

23. Maintaining the population of a specific species or managing a community is a decision that is made by

    A. wildlife managers
    B. subsistence farmers

    C. deep ecologists
    D. economists

24. Why are amphibians more likely to be susceptible to environmental problems than mammals?

    A. Their offspring are born live and nursed by the mother.
    B. They have permeable skin and unprotected eggs.
    C. Toxins bioaccumulate in fur.
    D. They are bellwether species.

25. When numerous species disappear during a relatively short geologic time period, it is called:

    A. extinction
    B. mass extinction

    C. background extinction
    D. biological diversity

26. Which of the following is NOT a technique used by wildlife managers to control the stage of succession?

    A. Raising threatened organisms in captivity.
    B. Planting specific types of vegetation.
    C. Using controlled fires to burn undergrowth.
    D. Building artificial ponds.

27. The study of the traditional uses of plants by indigenous peoples.

    A.   Conservation biology   C. Forensic biology
    B.   Natural products   D. Ethnobotany

28. By destroying tropical rain forests and other complex ecosystems, we may reduce or eliminate species replacement through:

    A. biological diversity
    B. background extinction
    C. ecosystem management
    D. adaptive radiation

29. Which of the following is NOT an example of exploitation of endangered species?

    A. hunting walruses for their tusks.
    B. selling bear gallbladders to Asian medical markets.
    C. Poaching tigers.
    D. Culling elephant herds.

30. Which of the following is NOT an economic reason for preserving biodiversity?

    A. Ecosystems are inspirational.
    B. Animals provide food.
    C. Genetic reserves enhance domestic animal breeding.
    D. Plants provide medicines.

FILL IN:

1. In _____ _____, sperm collected from a suitable male of a rare species is used to artificially impregnate a female, perhaps located in another zoo in a different city or even in another country.

2. Many _____ _____ have a very limited natural range, which makes them particularly prone to extinction if their habitat is altered.

3. During the 19th and 20th centuries, many whale species were harvested to the point of _____ _____, meaning that so few remain that it is unprofitable to hunt them.

4. In _____ _____, a female of a rare species is treated with fertility drugs, which cause her to produce multiple eggs. Some of these eggs are collected, fertilized with

sperm, and surgically implanted into a female of a related but less rare species, who later gives birth to offspring of the rare species.

5. When the black-footed ferret was reintroduced on the Wyoming prairie, it was classified as a(n) _____, _____ _____ so that its reintroduction would not block ranching and mining in the area.

6. _____ , the death of a species, occurs when the last individual member of a species dies.

7. Many endangered species have a very limited natural range, which makes them particularly prone to extinction if their _____ is altered.

8. _____ is the eventual fate of all species, much as death is the eventual fate of all individuals.

9. _____ _____ are organisms that provide an early warning of environmental damage.

10. A(n) _____ _____ refers not only to any land mass surrounded by water but also to any isolated habitat that is surrounded by an expanse of unsuitable territory.

11. _____ _____ are introduced into new areas by natural means or by human activities.

12. _____ _____ _____ includes the establishment of parks and reserves, and concentrates on preserving biological diversity in nature through the identification and protection of sites with a great deal of diversity.

13. The conviction that all organisms have the right to exist and that humans should not cause the extinction of other organisms is known as _____ _____ .

14. Conservationists would like to see the _____ _____ _____ strengthened in such a way as to preserve whole ecosystems and maintain complete biological diversity rather than attempting to save individual endangered species.

15. _____ _____ _____ involves conserving biological diversity in human-controlled settings.

16. _____ _____ is the removal of live commercially important organisms from nature.

17. One hundred twenty eight countries participate in the _____ of wild flora and fauna, which bans hunting, capturing, and selling of endangered or threatened species.

18. In addition to conserving biological diversity worldwide, the _____ _____ _____ seeks to preserve the vital ecosystem processes on which all life depends for survival and to develop sustainable uses of organisms and the ecosystems that they comprise.

19. _____ _____ are substances taken directly from organisms that can be used for drugs and other beneficial purposes.

20. Wildlife ranching, the cultivation of wild species, is also known as _____ _____.

21. In _____ _____ the target organism is killed for profit.

22. _____ _____ is the study and protection of biological diversity.

23. Long-term survival and _____ depend on genetic diversity, so its loss adds to the risk of extinction for endangered and threatened species as compared to species that have greater genetic variability.

24. When extinction is less imminent but the population of a particular species is quite low, the species is said to be _____.

25. The number and variety of organisms is referred to as _____ _____.

26. The incorporation of genes from one organism into an entirely different species, known as _____ _____, makes it possible to use the genetic resources of organisms on a much wider scale than had earlier been possible.

27. Under the conditions of the _____ _____ _____ produced by the 1992 Earth Summit, each signatory nation must inventory its own biodiversity and develop a national conservation strategy, a detailed plan for managing and preserving the biological diversity of that specific country.

28. The variation among organisms is referred to as biological diversity or _____.

29. A species is _____ when its numbers are so severely reduced that it is in danger of becoming extinct without human intervention.

30. The evolution of a large number of related species from an ancestral organism is called _____ _____.

31. During the course of their annual migrations, which usually follow established routes called _____, ducks must have areas in which to rest and feed.

32. Biological diversity also includes _____ _____ which is the variety of interactions among organisms in natural communities.

33. Where elephant populations are too large, they must be reduced by _____, which is killing the older, less fit elephants.

34. The area in which a particular species is found is its _____.

35. _____, the introduction of a foreign, or exotic, species into an area where it is not native, often upsets the balance among the organisms living in that area.

36. At certain periods in the earth's history, maybe five or six times, there has been a second kind of extinction, _____ _____, in which numerous species disappeared during a relatively short period of geological time.

37. _____ _____ includes the regulation of hunting and fishing and the management of food, water, and habitat for wildlife populations.

38. During the span of time in which organisms have occupied Earth, there has been a continuous, low-level extinction of species, known as _____ _____ .

39. The variety within a species as represented by the different colored kernels in maize is called _____ _____.

40. _____ _____ is the number of different species.

41. Efforts to preserve biological diversity in nature are known as ____ _____ _____.

TRUE OR FALSE:

1. True   False   Fishes with commercial or sport value have not been overexploited to the point of extinction.

2. True   False   Once an organism is extinct, it can never exist again.

3. True   False   Sometimes species become endangered or extinct as a result of deliberate efforts to eradicate or control their numbers.

4. True   False   It is unlikely that any as-yet-unknown species may someday provide us with products.

5. True   False   Ex situ conservation is the identification and protection of sites with a great deal of biological diversity.

6. True   False   A reduction in biological diversity is occurring worldwide, but the problem is most critical in temperate areas.

7. True   False   Controlling the stage of ecological succession of an area's vegetation encourages the presence of certain animals and discourages others.

8. True   False   Many African farmers do not like wildlife because wildlife kill or spread disease among cattle and trample crops.

9. True   False   Perhaps the most important advantage of seed banks is that plants stored in this manner remain stagnant in an evolutionary sense.

10. True   False   Extinction is a natural biological process.

11. True   False   Genetic engineering depends on a broad base of genetic diversity from which it can obtain genes.

12. True   False   It is more cost-effective to maintain natural habitats so that species will never become endangered in the first place.

13. True   False   Habitats that are left "totally" undisturbed and natural are degraded by human-produced acid rain, ozone depletion, and climate change.

14. True   False   Islands are insulated from the introduction of exotic species.

15. True   False   A political commitment to protect organisms is unnecessary because many immediate or short-term economic benefits are obtained from conserving species.

16. True   False   Wildlife ranching, besides being financially attractive, is less harmful to the environment than traditional agriculture.

17. True   False   Extinction represents a permanent loss in biological diversity.

PEOPLE WHO MATTER:

1. Senator John Glenn, along with other Senators and Representatives from the Great Lakes region, introduced the "Nonindigenous Aquatic Nuisance Act of 1990." This legislation was signed into law by President Bush in November 1990. The law was drafted in response to the invasion of the Great Lakes by the exotic species, the zebra mussel. It is thought that this species was unintentionally introduced to Lake St. Claire by a ship unloading cargo from a port on the Baltic Sea. At the time the legislation was introduced, this species was spreading rapidly, clogging up water lines and pipes in factories, water

treatment plants, and boat engines. The law has two parts. One is to look for ways to control the zebra mussels in the lakes. The second part requires all ships entering the Great Lakes to exchange their ballast water at sea. (Ballast water is the millions of gallons of water that ships take into special tanks to stabilize them when they are loading and unloading cargo.) Why do you think that the second part of the law was written? Will it have any effect on controlling the zebra mussel population in the Lakes?

MAKING CONNECTIONS:

1. You have been given freshly collected soil samples from two different areas under consideration for inclusion in a protected nature reserve. What information can you obtain from these samples that will help you make a decision about which area to protect?

MAKING DECISIONS:

1. An exotic pet shop in your community caught on fire and burned. In the process of fighting the fire, a number of "pets" were released and not recaptured. The owners of the shop assured the members of the community that these South American species could not survive the harsh winters in your region and advised you not to worry about the few organisms still missing. Those still on the missing list include five rodents similar to a hamster, a parrot, and two lizards. What are the potential problems associated with the release of these organisms into the ecosystem in your community?

2. It has been two years since the pet shop burned in your community. Now the hospital and doctors in your community are seeing a large number of children who have been bitten by brown furry animals they mistake for an escaped hamster. So far, none of the children has contracted any illnesses from these animals, but the potential exists, and the parents of your community are concerned. After doing research on these organisms in their native habitat, you learn that there is a small cat-like mammal that is the natural predator of these rodents. Some members of your community would like to release these "cats" in the neighborhood to eat the rodents. Is this a good idea? What problems could result from introducing this species?

3. Can you think of situation in which the reintroduction of a species that is naturally extinct could be perceived as a problem?

DOING SCIENCE:

1. The National Cancer Institute has guaranteed the government of Malaysia part of the profits of any drugs obtained from organisms in Malaysian rainforests. Malaysia has an economic incentive to preserve its remaining rainforests, because if a cure for cancer or

AIDs exists there, Malaysia could earn millions of dollars. How can the Malaysian government help find potential cures within the rainforests?

CHECKING WHAT YOU KNOW: (HINT)

MULTIPLE CHOICE: (HINT)

1. C	9. D	17. C	25. B
2. A	10. B	18. D	26. A
3. A	11. A	19. A	27. D
4. A	12. B	20. D	28. D
5. D	13. B	21. B	29. D
6. D	14. B	22. D	30. A
7. C	15. B	23. A	
8. D	16. D	24. B	

FILL IN: (HINT)

1. artificial insemination
2. endangered species
3. commercial extinction
4. embryo transfer
5. experimental, nonessential species
6. Extinction
7. habitat
8. Extinction
9. Bellwether species
10. Island
11. Exotic species
12. In situ conservation
13. deep ecology
14. Endangered Species Act
15. Ex situ conservation
16. Commercial harvest
17. Convention on International Trade in Endangered Species (CITES)
18. World Conservation Strategy
19. Natural products
20. game farming
21. commercial hunting
22. Conservation biology
23. evolution
24. threatened
25. biological diversity,
26. genetic engineering
27. biological diversity treaty
28. biodiversity
29. endangered
30. adaptive radiation
31. flyways
32. ecosystem diversity
33. culling
34. range
35. Biotic pollution
36. mass extinction
37. Wildlife management
38. background extinction
39. genetic diversity
40. Species diversity
41. in situ conservation

TRUE OR FALSE: (HINT)

1. false	6. false	11. true	16. true
2. true	7. true	12. true	17. true
3. true	8. true	13. true	
4. false	9. false	14. false	
5. false	10. true	15. false	

PEOPLE WHO MATTER: (HINT)

1. The second part of the law was written as an attempt to find ways to prevent the future accidental introduction of other species into the Great Lakes through the release of ballast water. This provision of the law will only affect the population of zebra mussels in the Lakes to the extent that it should reduce the likelihood that more zebra mussels will be introduced. It cannot have any impact on the organisms already present.

MAKING CONNECTIONS: (HINT)

1. Looking at soil can tell you a lot about an ecosystem. Refer to chapter 14 for details of soil characteristics. Some things you can look for:
- How much organic material is present? -- Food chain issue.
- Is there evidence of pollutants or toxins in the soil?
- How many different species of bacteria, fungi, spores, arthropods, and worms can you find in the samples?

MAKING DECISIONS: (HINT)

1. These organisms are not native to the ecosystem in which you live. They are exotic or foreign species. If they can survive and establish a population, they can disrupt the natural ecosystem. They can compete with native species for food, habitat, and resources. In spite of quarantine laws, they could introduce diseases into the native populations. They could prey upon native species. They could become an inappropriate food source for native species. Often the species most vulnerable to foreign invaders are those species that are already rare, threatened, or endangered.

2. You must first consider what problems adding a second exotic species to the ecosystem will cause. Everything identified in question 1 applies here. In addition, what will it prey on after the exotic rodents are gone or reduced? Another problem to consider is whether or not this species can survive in your ecosystem. Simply because one species was successful does not mean that the second will be. You should try to learn if these "cats" can survive long enough to eliminate the rodent problem. If not, how many do

you need to import to accomplish the task? What are the ethics of taking these organisms from their native habitat? What will capturing these organisms do to their native ecosystem?

3. Read pages 11-12 "Reintroducing Wolves to Yellowstone." What is the position of the ranchers in the area?

DOING SCIENCE: (HINT)

1. Many medications that have come from plant species have been identified because the plant was used medicinally. Scientists identify a plant that had been used to treat a specific symptom. They then try to isolate the component of the plant responsible for the effect. Once the component has been identified, they do all the standard tests necessary to get approval for the use of any medicine. They must demonstrate through the collection of data in animals and eventually clinical trials in human beings that the compound is responsible for the effect AND that there are no harmful side-effects from use of the compound. Often there must be a trade-off between minimal side-effects and a beneficial treatment much as we do risk-benefit analysis of environmental problems. For example, in treating cancer, there are many nasty side-effects, but elimination of the cancer is so desirable that the side-effects can be tolerated.

One approach to identifying beneficial organisms in the Malaysian rain forest would be to send ethnobotanists into the forest to study the plants currently being used medicinally.

A more daunting approach would be to systematically identify the natural products made in the plants found in the forest. Since there is such a diversity, it would be reasonable to try to start with the plants that are closely related to species with known medicinal functions. A catalogue of all the species in the forest would be very useful as well.

CHAPTER 17 -- LAND RESOURCE AND CONSERVATION

LEARNING THE LANGUAGE:

1972 Clean Water Act
abiotic
alpine tundra
atmosphere
biogeochemical cycles
biological diversity
carrying capacity
charcoal
clearcutting
coastal wetland
commercial harvest
deforestation
desert
desertification
dust bowl
ecosystem
ecosystem management
Emergency Wetlands Restoration Act
endangered species
Endangered Species Act
forest management
freshwater wetland
habitat
hydrologic cycle
monoculture

nonurban land
overgrazing
range
rangeland
rural land
salvage logging
secondary succession
sedimentation
selective cutting
shelterwood cutting
slash-and-burn agriculture
soil erosion
subsistence agriculture
sustainable development
threatened species
transpiration
tropical rain forest
tundra
urbanization
watershed
wetland
wilderness
wildlife corridor
wise-use movement

CHECKING WHAT YOU KNOW:

MULTIPLE CHOICE:

1. _____ protects natural resources and habitats along the Atlantic, Pacific, and Gulf of Mexico coasts.

    A. The National Marine Sanctuary Program
    B. The Bureau of Land Management
    C. The U.S. Fish and Wildlife Service
    D. The Wetland Reserve Program

2. The predominant vegetation in rangelands is:

    A. trees.   B. ferns.   C. grasses.   D. shrubs.

3. The key difference between the approach of the Endangered Species Act and ecosystem management is that ecosystem management:

   A. seeks to help endangered species.
   B. seeks a management plan for the preservation of an endangered species.
   C. recognizes that the organism must interact with all aspects of its environment.
   D. requires federal officials to make the decisions.

4. In forests, how much water returns to the atmosphere through transpiration and evaporation?

   A. 25%   B. 50%   C. 75%   D. 100%

5. Which of the following represents a statement more likely to be made by an environmentalist than by a proponent of wise-use?

   A. Federal lands are overregulated.
   B. Federal lands should only be managed for economic growth and development.
   C. Federal lands should be available for human use.
   D. Federal lands should be managed to protect ecosystems.

6. The most common terrain to be safeguarded by the National Wilderness Preservation System is

   A. tundra.   B. deserts.   C. wetlands.   D. mountains.

7. Which of the following is NOT a function of a coastal wetland?

   A. Protects coastlines from erosion
   B. Prevents nutrient depletion in agricultural fields
   C. Reduces damage from hurricanes
   D. Supports a productive food web

9. The world's largest biome is the _____.

   A. tundra   C. temperate rain forest
   B. temperate grassland   D. boreal forest

10. How much land in the United States is privately held?

   A. 3%   B. 7%   C. 35%   D. 55%

11. When a forest is clearcut, the total amount of surface water that flows into rivers and streams
    _____.

    A. increases   B. decreases   C. stays the same

12. The temporary or permanent clearance of a forest is called _____.

    A. clearcutting   C. desertification
    B. deforestation   D. sustainable

13. Which of the following is NOT an environmental service provided by forests?

    A. habitat for wildlife   C. prevention of soil erosion
    B. protection of watersheds D. commercially important timber

14. Most of the land in the United States is

    A. rangeland and grassland. C. cropland
    B. forestland   D. urban and suburban

15. In _____ almost all of the trees except a scattering of desirable trees are cut. The remaining trees provide seeds for regeneration of the forest.

    A. seed tree cutting   C. selective cutting
    B. clearcutting   D. shelterwood cutting

16. Much of the improvement in the quality of federal lands can be attributed to _____ livestock being permitted to graze on them.

    A. more   B. less   C. the same amount of

17. Which of the following agencies of the U.S. government controls the greatest amount of land

    A. National Park Service   C. U.S. Forest Service
    B. U.S. Fish and Wildlife Service D. Bureau of Land Management

18. _____ which are being logged by clearcutting, are currently the primary source of the world's industrial wood and wood fiber.

A. Temperate rain forests   C. Taiga
B. Tropical rain forests   D. Boreal forests

19. _____ are found in tropical areas that have a sufficient amount of rain to support trees, but also have prolonged dry seasons.

A. Tropical rain forests   C. Tropical dry forests
B. Boreal forests   D. Scrub savannas

20. Which of the following is NOT a function of wetlands?

A. water purification   C. wildlife habitat
B. provide employment for millions of D. recharging groundwater
  people worldwide

FILL IN:

1. Keeping in mind that tropical deforestation is a complex problem, three agents-- _____ _____, commercial logging, and cattle ranching-- are thought to be the most immediate causes of deforestation.

2. Ecosystem management recognizes that organisms interact with one another and with their _____ environment (soil, water, and air).

3. Areas that have not been greatly disturbed by human activities are called _____.

4. Photosynthesis by trees removes large quantities of carbon dioxide from the _____ and fixes it into carbon compounds.

5. Melting snows in the highest portions of Utah's alpine _____ furnish 60 percent of the water in the state's streams, even during the hot days of summer.

6. Timber companies prefer _____ because it is the most cost-effective way to harvest trees and because relatively little road building has to be done to harvest a large number of trees.

7. In a biological cooling process called _____, water from the soil is absorbed by roots, transported through plants, and then evaporated from their leaves and stems.

8. Historically, tidal marshes and other _____ _____ have been regarded as wasteland, good only for breeding large populations of mosquitoes.

9. The lack of plant cover due to _____ in rangelands allows wind to erode the soil.

10. The overuse of rangelands or dry forests contributes to _____, the development of unproductive desert-like conditions on formerly productive land.

11. The loss of wetlands is legislatively controlled by a section of the _____.

12. Forests play an important role in the _____ _____ by returning most of the water that falls as precipitation to the atmosphere by transpiration.

13. _____ is the concentration of humans in cities.

14. Many tropical species have very limited _____ within a forest, so they are especially vulnerable to habitat modification and destruction.

15. _____ _____, in which enough food is produced by a family to feed itself, accounts for perhaps 60 percent of tropical deforestation.

16. The removal of all mature trees in an area over a period of time is known as _____ _____ .

17. _____ are lands that are transitional between aquatic and terrestrial ecosystems.

18. _____ _____ _____ agriculture done on a small scale with periods of 20 to 100 years between cycles is sustainable.

19. The _____ authorizes the Fish and Wildlife Service to designate and acquire critically important wetlands.

20. Tropical _____ may contribute to an increase in global temperature by causing a release of stored carbon into the atmosphere as carbon dioxide, which in turn enables the air to retain heat.

21. The _____ _____ of a rangeland is the maximum number of animals the rangeland plants can sustain.

22. Deforestation results in decreased soil fertility and increased _____ _____ .

23. Forests that are intensively managed for _____ _____ have little species diversity.

24. In _____ , the older, mature trees are selectively harvested from time to time, and the forest regenerates itself naturally.

25. _____ _____ _____ is the predominate biome in places with 200 or more centimeters (at least 79 inches) of annual precipitation.

26. _____ is made by partially burning wood in a large kiln from which air is excluded.

27. Soil erosion can cause an increase in the _____ of waterways, which can harm downstream fisheries.

28. _____ , also called even-age harvesting, is the removal of all trees from an area.

29. Forests play an essential role in regulating global _____ _____ such as those for carbon and nitrogen.

30. _____ occurs when so much of the plant is consumed by the grazing animals that it cannot recover, and it dies.

31. Expanding forests are the result of _____ _____ on abandoned farms, commercial planting, and government protection.

32. _____ _____ are protected zones that connect unlogged areas.

33. People who support the _____ _____ _____ think that the government has too many regulations protecting the environment and that property owners should be freed from the requirements of environmental laws.

34. During _____ _____ trees that are weakened by insects, disease, or fire are harvested.

35. The higher elevations of mountains, above the tree line, which have a distinctive ecosystem are known as _____ _____ .

36. In addition to being highly productive areas, _____ _____ protect coastlines from erosion and reduce damage from hurricanes.

37. Most people living in sparsely populated _____ _____ have jobs directly connected with natural resources.

38. Forests are effective _____ because they absorb, hold, and slowly release water; this provides a more regulated flow, even during dry periods, and helps to control floods and droughts.

39. _____ or rural lands include wilderness, forests, grasslands, and wetlands.

40. _____are grasslands, in both temperate and tropical climates, that serve as important areas of food production for humans by providing fodder for domestic animals such as cattle, sheep, and goats.

41. _____ _____ recognizes that organisms interact with one another and with their abiotic environment (soil, water, and air).

42. After a species has been declared endangered, the _____ _____ _____ requires that federal officials design a plan to aid in the species' recovery.

43. A _____ is an area covered by essentially one crop such as corn in a field or pine trees in a managed forest.

44. The predominant vegetation of _____ includes grasses, forbs (small herbaceous plants other than grasses), and shrubs.

True and False:

1.　　True　False　The only ecological benefit of wetlands is to provide food for migratory waterbirds.

2.　　True　False　One of the best ways to maintain biological diversity and to protect endangered and threatened species is by preserving or restoring the natural areas to which these organisms are adapted.

3.　　True　False　Subsistence farmers go into the forest, which they clear and sell for wood products and furniture.

4.　　True　False　Pollution is not a problem in national parks.

5.　　True　False　Clearcutting over wide areas is ecologically sound.

6.　　True　False　Rangelands are important in the production of domestic animals.

7.　　True　False　Most precipitation is lost from deforested areas as runoff.

8.　　True　False　Many rangeland plants have fibrous root systems that hold the soil in place.

9.　　True　False　One of the best ways to maintain biological diversity and to protect endangered and threatened species is by preserving or restoring the natural areas to which these organisms are adapted.

10.   True   False   Agriculture, pollution, engineering (such as dams), and urbanization do not threaten wetlands.

11.   True   False   Deforestation contributes to the extinction of many species.

12.   True   False   The United States is attempting to prevent any new net loss of wetlands by conserving existing wetlands and restoring some of those that have been lost.

PEOPLE WHO MATTER:

1. Table 17-4 is a list of edangered ecosystems in the United States. Choose the ecosystem from this list that is closest to where you live or that closely resembles an ecosystem where you live. Identify what environmental problems are faced by this ecosystem and who represents the factions involved in managing or protecting this ecosystem. Who are the people who matter to your local ecosystem?

2. Who is your local Senator or Representative? What do they think about funding for the Fish and Wildlife Service or a pending piece of environmental legislation?

MAKING CONNECTIONS:

1. Why does the protection of wild horses and burros have environmental drawbacks?

2. Examine Figure 17-19. If only 0.8% of the land worldwide is developed for human use, then why is there such a big deal about human impact on the planet?

MAKING DECISIONS:

1. The Bureau of Land Management manages an Adopt-a-Horse program. What are the two goals of managing the wild horse and burro populations?

2. Plug the words Bureau of Land Management and Adopt-a-Horse into any search engine. Two sites you will probably encounter are:

http://www.ecis.com/~whl/pag/whbnews.html

http://www.mcs.net/~rogers/globe/horsey.html

Check these sites out or find any other sites that interest you. What problems do they say exist with the Adopt-a-Horse program? How credible are these sites? What are their sources? If this topic concerns you, how will you act upon this information?

3. Examine Table 17-3 is a list of the top 12 farm areas threatened by population growth and urban/suburban spread. What questions would you want to ask before prioritizing such a list?

4. Three local landowners in your community share control over a local wetland. What can your community do to influence how they manage this natural resource?

CHECKING WHAT YOU KNOW: (HINT)

MULTIPLE CHOICE: (HINT)

1. A	6. D	11. B	16. D
2. C	7. B	12. D	17. D
3. C	8. D	13. B	18. C
4. C	9. D	14. A	19. B
5. D	10. A	15. B	

FILL IN: (HINT)

1. subsistence agriculture
2. abiotic
3. wilderness
4. atmosphere
5. tundra
6. clearcutting
7. transpiration
8. coastal wetlands
9. overgrazing
10. desertification
11. 1972 Clean Water Act
12. hydrologic cycle
13. Urbanization
14. ranges
15. Subsistence agriculture
16. shelterwood cutting
17. Wetlands
18. Slash-and-burn
19. Emergency Wetlands Resources Act of 1986
20. deforestation
21. carrying capacity
22. soil erosion

23. commercial harvest
24. selective cutting
25. Tropical rain forest
26. Charcoal
27. sedimentation
28. Clearcutting
29. biogeochemical cycles
30. Overgrazing
31. secondary succession
32. Wildlife corridors
33. wise-use movement
34. salvage logging
35. alpine tundra
36. coastal wetlands
37. rural lands (or nonurban lands)
38. watersheds
39. Nonurban
40. Rangelands
41. Ecosystem management
42. Endangered Species Act
43. monoculture
44. rangelands

TRUE OR FALSE: (HINT)

1. false
2. true
3. false
4. false
5. false
6. true
7. true

8. *true*
9. *true*
10. *false*
11. *true*
12. *true*

PEOPLE WHO MATTER: (HINT)

1. This is a local research project. You must first identify an ecosystem close to home. For example, I live in an area that used to be a major swamp before it was drained. There are few natural wetlands left in this region. Agencies and individuals involved in this issue include local politicians, farming organizations, water and soil conservation districts, and local and national environmental organizations. I am able to identify faculty from the local university and school system who are leaders in wetlands restoration issues. I can also identify members of the county Board of Commissioners who have a stake in the issue. By attending meetings, I can get to know these people who matter within my community, and I can begin to find ways to influence local activities that relate to my issue of concern.

2. Identify your Senators or Representative by using the phonebook, the internet, or your local library. Find out the name of the legislative assistant who handles environmental issues. Write a short letter directly to this individual asking for your Congressman's position on specific pieces of legislation.

MAKING CONNECTIONS: (HINT)

1. Wild horses and burros are nonindigenous species. They compete with the native species in the range they occupy. Through overgrazing they can cause serious habitat destruction. Preservation of these species for political and historical reasons must be balanced with the detrimental effects a nonnative species can have on the environment.

2. The best answer to this question is to remember that pollution does not respect any human imposed barrier. It can cross arbitrary human boundaries. Review what you have learned about the atmosphere and the hydrosphere. In examining both of these realms, you can gain an understanding of how human activity in one area can adversely affect remote wilderness. Also, consider the activities that support human life: mining, agriculture, ranching, extraction of raw materials, consumption of water. All of these activities exert an influence on an area much greater than that actually developed for the human use.

MAKING DECISIONS: (HINT)

1. Wild horse and burro populations are considered part of the American cultural heritage and as such are protected species. One goal is to maintain these animals in the wild much the same as the Endangered Species Act protects endangered species. The second goal is to prevent these populations, which are not native, from overgrazing and harming the land on which they depend.

2. Several problems have been identified with the Adopt-a-Horse program. Critics are concerned about what happens to the animals after they are adopted. Many anomals go to good homes and are treated well. Many other animals end up in abusive environments or end up in the slaughter house.

As you check out web-sites, you must be aware of who is providing the information and what their agenda might be. The information you find may be false, it may be misleading, it may be incomplete. You need to check out several sources and confirm the information you obtain before you make concrete decisions to act. The first site listed in this question is produced by a group of individuals interested in all aspects of ownership of horses. They use the BLM as part of their sources. They also have input from site visitors. They say that they monitor the input. This site is linked to the homepage of the organization as well as other sites of interest. The second site in the question leads to a dead end. Global watch is at the top of the page, and sources such as the Associated Press are cited. However, there is no information about the individual or organization available without further use of a search engine on the visitor's part. There are no email links or links to other pages. A further investigation of this site (by deleting information at the end of the address until a homepage was reached) provides little more information about the individual or organization responsible. Other articles at this website do cite names and phone numbers for more information.

While the information in both sites may be correct, it is essential that the sources of the information be specified or that the information be confirmed. One should question information obtained through such sources before acting.

3. Lists such at the one in Table 17-3 must be generated after a gathering of facts. Likely questions that lead to the production of this prioritized list include:
- How much farmland has existed here historically?
- How much farmland has been developed for human use?
- At what rate is farmland being converted for human use?
- How much farmland is needed to support existing populations?

4.
- Educate them about the benefits of wetlands.
- Buy the property through public means or private foundations.
- Change zoning laws to restrict development.
- Change tax laws to restrict development or to favor protection.

CHAPTER 18 -- FOOD RESOURCES: A CHALLENGE FOR AGRICULTURE

LEARNING THE LANGUAGE:

alternative agriculture
antioxidants
aquaculture
bycatch
calorie
cancer
carbohydrates
cell respiration
domesticated
essential amino acids
famine
food additive
Food and Drug Administration (FDA)
food chain
free-range
genetic diversity
genetic engineering
germplasm
green revolution
habitat
hedgerows
herbicide
herbicide resistance
high-input agriculture
industrialized agriculture
inorganic fertilizer
insecticide

International Plant Genetics Resources
  Institute
kwashiorkor
lipids
malnutrition
marasmus
mariculture
minerals
mopani
natural foods
nomadic herding
open management
organic agriculture
Organic Food Production Act of 1990
overnutrition
pesticide
polyculture
preservatives
protein
shifting agriculture
slash-and-burn agriculture
soil erosion
subsistence agriculture
sustainable agriculture
undernutrition
vitamins
world grain carryover stocks

CHECKING WHAT YOU KNOW:

MULTIPLE CHOICE:

1. Sugars and starches are examples of

    A. carbohydrates
    B. fats and lipids

    C. proteins
    D. nucleic acids

2. Essential amino acids and vitamins are added to foods to make them _____

    A. more nutritious than they would be naturally.
    B. taste better than they would naturally.
    C. look better than they would naturally.
    D. remain fresher longer than they would naturally.

3. People who consume fewer nutrients than they need are said to be _____.

   A. malnourished
   B. undernourished

   C. overnourished
   D. metabolized

4. People who consume more calories than they need are said to be _____.

   A. malnourished
   B. undernourished

   C. overnourished
   D. metabolized

5. People who consume fewer calories than they need are said to be _____.

   A. malnourished
   B. undernourished

   C. overnourished
   D. metabolized

6. Butylated hydroxyanisole (BHA) and butylated hydroxytoluene (BHT) are examples of _____.

   A. antioxidants
   B. food additives

   C. coloring agents
   D. pesticides

7. _____ is/are the use of a variety of techniques to maximize control of pests and minimize the environmental impacts.

   A. Biological controls
   B. Agricultural modifications

   C. Genetic modification
   D. Integrated pest management

8. Which of the following would be an appropriate accompaniment to a meal of rice to insure the proper amount and types of amino acids?

   A. lettuce   B. apples   C. tofu   D. corn

9. A meat-eater gets no more than about _____ calorie(s) of energy from every 100 calories fixed by the plants that were consumed by the cows.

   A. 1   B. 10   C. 100   D. 1000

10. Which of the following is NOT found in natural foods?

A. organic fruits and vegetables
B. unrefined sugars
C. range-fed animals
D. hydrogenated oils

11. The average human adult must consume enough food to get approximately _____ kilocalories per day.

A. 1600   B. 2000   C. 2600   D. 3000

12. Nitrates and nitrites are used

A. as mineral supplements.
B. as vitamins.
C. to cure meats.
D. to raise cattle.

13. A vegetarian will get no more than about _____ calorie(s) of energy from every 100 calories that were fixed by plants in photosynthesis.

A. 1   B. 10   C. 100   D. 1000

14. Why is a vegetarian able to extract energy from the environment more efficiently than a person who eats meat?

A. There is little loss of energy as you move up the energy pyramid. Therefore, a meat eater is really as efficient as a vegetarian.
B. Most of the energy is lost as you move up the energy pyramid. The plants capture solar energy and the vegetarian eats the plants, getting more of the original energy from the sun than the meat eater.
C. Protein is the important thing to observe when looking at food chains. There is more protein in meat than in plants.
D. Actually, it is the decomposers who can get the best energy conversion because they are eating dead stuff.

15. A _____ is any living thing that successfully competes with humans for food, space, or other "essential" needs.

A. herbivore
B. secondary consumer
C. pest
D. parasite

16. Organic farming _____ than conventional farming practices.

    A. is more labor-intensive
    B. produces greater food quantities

    C. costs less
    D. uses more fossil fuel

17. Alternative agriculture does NOT rely on:

    A. natural predator-prey relationships
    B. large quantities of chemical pesticides

    C. birds and other insect predators
    D. breeding disease-resistant crops

18. Which of the following food chains represents the actual path of energy in your lunch of a fish sandwich?

    A. perch ---> minnow ---> human
    B. human ---> perch ---> algae ---> minnow
    C. zooplankton ---> minnow ---> human ---> perch
    D. algae ---> zooplankton ---> minnow ---> perch ---> human

19. Which of the following is found in sufficient quantity in a diet that consists primarily of rice?

    A. calories   B. protein   C. minerals   D. lipids

20. Which of the following is NOT a large source of energy for subsistence farming?

    A. fossil fuels   B. humans   C. animals

21. _____ are the subunits that make up proteins.

    A. Carbohydrates
    B. Monosaccarides

    C. Amino acids
    D. Oils

22. Which of the following is NOT a reason we add chemicals to food?

    A. attract insects
    B. make it taste better

    C. preserve it
    D. make it look better

23. The FDA regulates food additives. What does FDA stand for?

    A. Food and Drug Administration
    B. Federal Drug Act

    C. Federal Disease Administration
    D. Food, Drugs, Alcohol

24. Which of the following is NOT a seafood that may be grown by aquaculture?

    A. seaweeds   B. tuna   C. shrimp   D. oysters

25. Which of the following is NOT a part of alternative agriculture?

    A. growing the same crop plants each season.
    B. breeding disease-resistant crop plants
    C. maintaining animal health
    D. maintaining biological diversity on the farm

26. When plants and animals are _____, genetic diversity is lost.

    A. wild
    B. domesticated

    C. eaten
    D. propagated

27. Which of the following is NOT stored by the human body for later use?

    A. amino acids   B.   carbohydrates   C.   lipids

28. People who eat worms do so because

    A. Worms are a good source of protein
    B. Nobody likes them
    C. It is accepted in the common culture of the United States
    D. Worms have no nutritive value and should never be consumed.

FILL IN:

1. _____ are the amounts of rice, wheat, corn, and other grains remaining from previous harvests, as estimated at the start of a new harvest.

2. _____ are complex organic molecules that are required in very small quantities by living cells.

3. _____ _____ produces high yields of food but causes serious environmental problems such as soil erosion and pollution.

4. _____ _____, also called sustainable or low-input agriculture, relies on beneficial biological processes and environmentally friendly chemicals instead of chemical pesticides.

5. The cultivation of marine organisms is a type of aquaculture called _____ .

6. The _____ is charged with the responsibility of monitoring food additives.

7. Many nations have a policy of _____ , in which all fishing boats of that country are given unrestricted access to fishes in national waters.

8. _____ _____ contributes to species' long-term survival by providing the variation that enables each population to adapt to changing environmental conditions.

9. _____ _____, in which livestock is supported by land that is too arid for successful crop growth, is another type of land-intensive subsistence agriculture.

10. _____ are large, complex molecules composed of repeating subunits called amino acids.

11. Some alternative farmers—those who practice _____ _____ --use no pesticide chemicals.

12. _____ _____ are any foods that are not highly processed and do not contain synthetic preservatives, artificial colors and flavors, refined sugars and synthetic sweeteners, or hydrogenated oils.

13. Eating food in excess of that required is called _____ .

14. Fish farming, or _____, is more closely related to agriculture on land than it is to the fishing industry.

15. Perhaps the greatest potential contribution of _____ _____ in the animal arena is in the production of vaccines against disease organisms that harm agricultural animals.

16. There is evidence that wheat was _____ from wild grasses as early as 10,000 years ago.

17. _____ is the ability to take a specific gene from one cell and place it into another cell, where it is expressed.

18. _____ are rows of bushes between fields that provide a habitat for birds and other insect predators.

19. Some scientists are genetically engineering _____ into crop plants so that when they apply herbicides, only the weeds die and not the crops.

20. _____ , organic molecules such as sugars and starches, are important primarily because they are metabolized readily by the body in cell respiration, a process in which the energy of organic molecules is transferred to adenosine triphosphate (ATP).

21. _____ is a traditional form of subsistence agriculture in which several different crops are grown at the same time.

22. One high-protein food in South Africa is _____ which are caterpillars of the emperor moth.

23. _____ _____ causes a decline in soil fertility, downstream sediment pollution, and water and soil pollution from pesticides and fertilizers.

24. The _____ in Rome, Italy, is the scientific organization that oversees plant germplasm collections worldwide.

25. Proteins are metabolized by the body in _____ _____ to release energy, which is transferred to ATP.

26. Crop failures caused by drought, war, flood, or some other catastrophic event may result in _____ , a severe food shortage.

27. _____ _____ are chemicals that enhance the taste, color, or texture of the food; improve its nutrition; reduce spoilage and prolong shelf life; or maintain the food's consistency.

28. Because so many fishes are concentrated in a relatively small area, _____ produces wastes that can pollute the adjacent water and harm other organisms.

29. Cattle and chickens that are labeled _____ _____, or naturally raised, are raised in open pastures or fields rather than in cramped pens and are not treated with antibiotics or hormones.

30. _____ _____ also called slash-and-burn agriculture, involves clearing small patches of tropical forest to plant crops.

31. Everyone acknowledges that the chemicals in our foods (i.e., food additives) do not pose anywhere near the threat of _____ that smoking does.

32. _____ _____ _____, also called industrialized agriculture, produces high yields of food per unit of farmland area, but not without costs such as soil degradation and an increase in pesticide resistance in agricultural pests.

33. _____ (a native word in Ghana, meaning "displaced child") is malnutrition resulting from protein deficiency.

34. _____, a diverse group of organic molecules that includes fats and oils, are metabolized by cell respiration to provide the body with a high level of energy.

35. The production of more food per acre of cropland by using new, high-yielding crop varieties and modern cultivation methods has been called the _____ _____ .

36. _____ are inorganic elements, such as iron and calcium, that are essential for the normal functioning of the human body.

37. Crop rotation, conservation tillage, and contour plowing help control _____ _____ and maintain soil fertility

38. Marasmus (from the Greek work marasmos, meaning "a wasting away") is progressive emaciation caused by a diet low in both total _____ and protein.

39. According to guidelines established by the _____, organic foods are crops that are grown in soil that has been free of chemical fertilizers and pesticides for at least three years.

40. Unwanted fishes, dolphins, and sea turtles, captured by commercial fishermen are collectively known as _____.

41. People who receive fewer _____ than they need are said to be undernourished.

42. Food additives that prevent oxidation are called _____ and include butylated hydroxyanisole (BHA) and butylated hydroxytoluene (BHT).

43. Human cells lack the ability to synthesize the eight amino acids called _____ _____ _____ .

44. In _____, certain modern agricultural techniques are carefully combined with traditional farming methods.

45. The lower _____ of domesticated plants and animals increases the likelihood that they will succumb to new strains of disease organisms.

46. Sodium propionate and potassium sorbate are two examples of _____, which are chemicals added to food to retard the growth of bacteria and fungi that cause food spoilage.

TRUE OR FALSE:

1. True   False   When plant and animal proteins in food are digested, the body absorbs the carbohydrates, which are then reassembled in different orders to form human proteins.

2. True   False   According to the Environmental Protection Agency, agricultural chemicals such as fertilizers and pesticides are the single largest cause of water pollution in the United States.

3. True   False   The problem with a vegetarian diet is usually not lack of protein, but obtaining the proper balance of essential amino acids.

4. True   False   Alternative agriculture tries to decrease biological diversity on farms as a way to minimize pest problems.

5. True   False   Because organic farming is more labor intensive, it produces more food than conventional agriculture.

6. True   False   One of the most important limits on aquaculture's potential is the identification of aquatic animals to domesticate.

7. True   False   Genetic engineering could produce food plants that would be more nutritious because they would contain all the essential amino acids.

8. True   False   Animal production has been increased by the use of antibiotics to build larger muscles.

9. True   False   The most important factor to examine when determining proper nutrition is the number of calories in the diet.

10. True   False   The amino acids essential for protein manufacture must be eaten together; it does no good to eat some of the essential amino acids for lunch and others for dinner.

11. True   False   Carbohydrates supply the body with the energy required to maintain life.

12. True   False   Inorganic fertilizer requires a great deal of energy to manufacture, so its production costs are tied closely to the price of energy.

13. True   False   Adults suffering from malnutrition are more susceptible to disease and have less strength to function productively than those who are well fed.

14. True   False   Fewer people die worldwide from undernutrition and malnutrition than from the starvation associated with famine.

15. True   False   Genetic engineering differs from traditional breeding methods in that desirable genes from any organism can be used, not just those from the species of the plant or animal that is being improved.

16. True   False   Many species have become endangered or threatened as a result of habitat loss caused by agriculture.

17. True   False   Overnutrition is most common among people in developing countries.

18. True   False   Some genetically engineered crops can benefit the environment because they reduce the use of chemical pesticides.

PEOPLE WHO MATTER:

1. Paul Hawken is actively involved in studying and understanding how businesses can grow while maintaining environmental sustainability. Read the interview with him on pages 430-431. What is natural capital? Are there ways to include the cost of natural capital into the cost of a product without using taxes? What would be the effect of including the cost of natural capital in food production? Do you agree with Mr. Hawken that natural capitalism will result in better products with less consumption of materials and energy? What do you think about natural capitalism?

MAKING CONNECTIONS:

1. One way to lessen the need for expensive inputs to agriculture is to find ways to enhance the function of natural systems. Describe biological nitrogen fixation and explain what agricultural chemical it replaces.

2. Examine the data in table 18-4. What does this tell you about the amount of fish caught in 1993 relative to the peak catch year? What is the obvious inference to make based on these data? What information is NOT contained in the data represented by the table?

3. Describe the food chain that is represented by your lunch.

4. One of the criticisms of some of the most successful organic farms is that they only function because they are surrounded by farmers using conventional methods of farming. What is the rationale behind this argument?

MAKING DECISIONS:

1. You are working for the United Nations. It is your job to bring famine relief to a village in a third world country. Because of arcane politics in the various donor nations, you may take a ship that contains 500 tons of rice, or you may fly in 200 tons of corn and 200 tons of beans. Which will you choose and why?

2. You are about to enter the voting booth to cast your ballot on an issue that could end all research in genetic engineering for the next ten years. List all of the benefits of genetic engineering. List all of the problems with genetic engineering. How will you vote?

DOING SCIENCE:

1. In question 4 under MAKING CONNECTIONS, you are asked about the impact that surrounding conventional farms have on organic farms. Design an experiment to test your hypothesis of whether or not there is an effect.

2. Examine the graph in figure 18-9. Is this sufficient data to support the statement "Worldwide fertilizer use declined from 1990 to 1994, but began to increase again in 1995"?

3. What would you do to find a biological control for a pest species destroying your cash crop?

CHECKING WHAT YOU KNOW: (HINT)

MULTIPLE CHOICE: (HINT)

1. A	9. A	17. B	25. A
2. A	10. D	18. D	26. B
3. A	11. C	19. A	27. A
4. C	12. C	20. A	28. A
5. B	13. B	21. C	29. A
6. B	14. B	22. A	
7. D	15. C	23. A	
8. C	16. A	24. B	

FILL IN: (HINT)

1. World grain carryover stocks
2. Vitamins
3. Industrialized agriculture
4. Alternative agriculture
5. mariculture
6. Food and Drug Administration (FDA)
7. open management
8. Genetic diversity
9. Nomadic herding
10. Proteins
11. organic agriculture
12. Natural foods
13. overnutrition
14. aquaculture
15. genetic engineering
16. domesticated
17. Genetic engineering
18. Hedgerows
19. herbicide resistance
20. Carbohydrates
21. Polyculture
22. mopani
23. Soil erosion
24. International Plant Genetics Resources Institute
25. cell respiration
26. famine
27. Food additives
28. aquaculture
29. free-range
30. Shifting agriculture

31. *cancer*
32. *High-input agriculture*
33. *Kwashiorkor*
34. *Lipids*
35. *green revolution*
36. *Minerals*
37. *Soil erosion*
38. *calories*
39. *Organic Food Production Act of 1990*
40. *bycatch*
41. *calories*
42. *antioxidants*
43. *essential amino acids*
44. *alternative agriculture*
45. *genetic diversity*
46. *preservatives*

TRUE OR FALSE: (HINT)

1. *false*
2. *true*
3. *true*
4. *false*
5. *false*
6. *true*
7. *true*
8. *false*
9. *false*
10. *true*
11. *true*
12. *true*
13. *true*
14. *false*
15. *true*
16. *true*
17. *false*
18. *true*

PEOPLE WHO MATTER: (HINT)

1. *According to Mr. Hawken, natural capital is the cost not only of natural resources, but of the services they provide. For example the value of the oxygen produced by the trees harvested to produce paper is part of the natural capital. Do you think that people will choose to buy products that include the cost of natural capital? How much more would you be willing to pay? Mr. Hawken states that although we pay $1.50 a gallon for gas, its real cost is $7.00. It is conceivable that a similar situation would exist with food. If the cost of gasoline included the natural capital costs, farmers would look for ways to reduce the consumption of gasoline. This could lead to more labor-intensive farming practices. How do you think that the amount of food produced in this system would be affected?*

MAKING CONNECTIONS: (HINT)

1. Refer to chapter 5 on the discussion of the nitrogen cycle. This is the process where nitrogen from the atmosphere is converted to biologically active forms. Bacteria are an important part of this process. Nitrogen is an essential fertilizer. Plants need nitrogen to make amino acids and other biologically active molecules. (The word amino in amino acid comes from a form of nitrogen.)

2. For every species represented in the table, the catch in 1993 was much less. The obvious inference is that the declining catch represents a decline in the number of fish in the total population. While this is probably the correct inference to make from the data, the table says nothing about the number of fishing vessels, weather that may have affected fishing, relative amounts of time spent fishing, or mandatory or voluntary limits on numbers of fish caught.

3. Figure out what was the highest level of the food chain you ate. If you are a vegetarian, then your food chain is simple....
Lettuce ---> human

If you ate meat, then you need to consider what that organism ate first....

plankton ---> fish -----> human

4. Some people believe that organic farms that are surrounded by conventional farms are protected from pest species because the adjacent lands where pesticides and herbicides are used have fewer pests. The distance between areas with pests and the organic farm is too great for the pests to traverse, and so few pests actually arrive on the crops in the organic farm.

MAKING DECISIONS: (HINT)

1. Your first instinct may be to choose the ship full of rice which is slower, but contains more food. Conversely you might choose the planes full of corn and beans because they are faster. Neither of these reasons would be best for the village. You should choose the corn and beans because they provide a balanced diet, including all the essential amino acids. A diet of rice alone will not prevent the villagers from dying. They will die of malnutrition rather than starvation.

2.

benefits	problems
crops with essential amino acids	*unknown effects of engineered organisms in environment*
less time than conventional breeding	*true of all technology*
more diversity as genes are moved between	*true of conventional breeding as well.*

species	
more food produced	need more/newer pesticides if resistant genes get into weeds
need less pesticides	

Consider all the pros and cons. Include all of your personal moral, religious, ethical beliefs on the list. Carefully consider the wording of the ballot issue. Does it exclude all research in genetics when you approve of gene therapy for curing human diseases? Does it exclude types of research you oppose? Are there loopholes that allow some to operate outside the system? Will the research go to an unregulated state or country? If so, who will benefit and who will be harmed? Ask yourself if the benefits are greater than the risk, make your decision, and cast your ballot.

DOING SCIENCE: (HINT)

1. Form your hypothesis.

a. If fewer pests reach a farm that is surrounded by conventional farms, then introducing pests to the farm should result in serious infestations.
b. If pests cannot cross the conventional farm to reach the organic farm, then reducing the distance between natural areas should increase the incidence of pest infestation on organic farms.
c. Organic farms that are not surrounded by conventional farms should have more pest problems than farms that are surrounded.

Design your experiment. Be sure to think about your controls.
a. Compare two organic fields or farms. Introduce pests into one and not into the other. Quantify numbers of pests and amount of damage.
b. Compare two organic fields or farms. Stop using pesticides on the fields adjacent to one, but not on the other. Quantify numbers of pests and amount of damage.
c. Find a number of organic farms. Some should be surrounded by conventional farms, and others should not. Quantify the numbers of pests and amount of damage.

2. Wait a few more years to see if this is a real trend, or if it is a small change comparable to what occurred around 1980.

3. Contact your local County Extension Agent. Alternatively, you will have to figure out where the pest species would normally live, what is its natural habitat. Observe it in that habitat and identify any predators. Conduct experiments to determine what the predator needs to survive in your fields. (Habitat requirements? Water? Nutrients?) Remember, the best biological control may not be a predator. It may be a parasite or disease-causing organism. Also, remember that you need to be sure that the biological control will not negatively affect desirable organisms on your farm. You will have to obtain permission from the state government (and possibly the federal government) to release any non-native species.

CHAPTER 19 -- AIR POLLUTION

LEARNING THE LANGUAGE:

air pollution
alcohol fuels
atmosphere
biological magnification
cancer
carbon dioxide
carbon oxides
Clean Air Acts
climate
coal gasification
cochlea
combustion
decibel
decibel-A
dust
dust domes
electrostatic precipitator
ethanol
fuel cells
global distillation effect
hydrocarbons
indoor air pollution
industrial smog
ionizing radiation

methane
mists
natural gas
nitrogen oxides
noise
ozone
particulate matter
photochemical smog
pollution control devices
population density
primary air pollutant
radon
secondary air pollutant
sick building syndrome
smog
solar energy
sound
stratosphere
sulfur oxides
sulfuric acid
thermal inversion
topography
troposphere
urban heat island

CHECKING WHAT YOU KNOW:

MULTIPLE CHOICE:

1. Which of the following activities is NOT yet regulated by the stringent smog laws in Los Angeles?

   A. paint vapors
   B. lawn mower emissions

   C. automotive fuel
   D. barbecue grills

2. The greatest source of carbon monoxide is _____.

   A. transportation
   B. power plants

   C. burning garbage
   D. factories

3. Which of the following is NOT a result of long-term exposure to toxic air pollutants?

   A. chronic obstructive pulmonary disease
   B. skin cancer
   C. asthma
   D. cardiovascular disease

4. _____ ozone is involved in global climate change.

   A. Tropospheric
   B. Stratospheric

   C. Thermospheric
   D. Mesospheric

5. Radon is a radioactive gas that can be found in rock, water, and cement. It is generally agreed to be carcinogenic. Which room in a house is likely to have the highest levels of radon gas?

   A. kitchen   B. bedroom   C. basement   D. attic

6. Which of the following is NOT an environmental problem that could be caused by or associated with running an electric race car?

   A. Electric cars are quieter than cars propelled by fossil fuel.
   B. The batteries contain lead that must be processed when they are made and disposed of when they no longer function.
   C. The electricity to charge the batteries must come from somewhere.
   D. The batteries are heavy and therefore reduce the distance the car can go between charges, which increases the amount of energy needed to run the car.

7. My friend Martin is flying a dollar store kite from the top of his hill. The kite is in the

   A. troposphere
   B. stratosphere

   C. mesosphere
   D. thermosphere

8. My friend Martin releases a weather balloon from a hill in his backyard. It reaches a height of 30 km, going past several 747 jets on its way up. The weather balloon reached what layer of the atmosphere?

A. troposphere.   C. thermosphere.
B. stratosphere.   D. mesosphere.

9. _____ air pollutants are potentially harmful as soon as they enter the atmosphere.

A. Secondary   B. Hazardous   C. Primary   D. Tertiary

10. Which of the following is NOT a reason Los Angeles is conducive to the formation of stable thermal inversions.

A. It is located on the San Andreas fault.
B. It has a sunny climate.
C. There is a high density of automobiles.
D. There is a large population.

11. As a result of increased particulate matter, urban areas receive _____ sunlight than rural areas.

A. less   B. the same amount   C. more

12. Remote regions are contaminated by volatile chemicals because

A. they occur there naturally in greater amounts than elsewhere.
B. they are dumped there by developed nations.
C. they are carried there by migrating birds.
D. they are transported there by the global distillation effect.

13. Which of the following alternative automotive fuels has no negative environmental consequences?

A. methane   C. alcohol
B. electricity   D. none of the above

14. As the sunlight gets stronger during the morning commute (between 7 and 10am), a brown cloud descends over Los Angeles. This is:

A. ozone   C. acid rain
B. photochemical smog   D. carbon monoxide

15. Which of the following is NOT a problem associated with sulfur oxides?

    A. global climate change
    B. metal corrosion

    C. acid deposition
    D. damage to stone

16. Which of the following will NOT reduce the radon concentration in a home?

    A. sealing concrete in basements
    B. ventilate crawl spaces

    C. ventilate attics
    D. ventilate basements

17. The National Research Council reviewed more than 500 studies on electromagnetic radiation and concluded that

    A. children living near power lines are at greater risk of getting leukemia.
    B. electromagnetic fields do not pose a significant health risk.
    C. public concern about electromagnetic fields is entirely justified.
    D. using a cellular phone causes cancer.

18. Photochemical smog is caused by a reaction between

    A. nitrogen oxides, hydrocarbons, and sunlight.
    B. sunlight, chlorine, and ozone.
    C. carbon dioxide in the troposphere and heat.
    D. sulfur compounds and rainwater.

19. The lag time between exposure to a carcinogen and development of cancer is

    A. 1-10 years
    B. 10-20 years

    C. 20-40 years
    D. 40-80 years

20. Which of the following forms of indoor air pollution has a biological cause?

    A. mothballs
    B. radon

    C. carbon monoxide
    D. mold

21. Which of the following is the loudest?

    A. vacuum cleaner
    B. dishwasher (very close)

    C. television
    D. motorcycle

22. Children are at a greater risk from air pollution because

    A. children are smaller.
    B. air pollution causes faster breathing.
    C. air pollution impedes lung development.
    D. children smoke more.

23. This chemical is commonly given off by new building materials, such as furniture, carpets, particle board, and from insulation.

    A. Ozone
    B. Lead
    C. Formaldehyde
    D. Nitrogen oxides

24. Technologies exist to control all forms of air pollution except

    A. ozone
    B. nitrogen oxides
    C. carbon dioxide
    D. sulfur dioxide

25. As a result of insulating our houses and sealing them up against the elements, we have also

    A. increased drafts and cold air gusts
    B. increased the amount of energy it takes to heat them
    C. trapped gases like radon
    D. all of these answers are correct

27. Under what conditions are electric cars cleaner than internal combustion engines?

    A. When the batteries are made with lead and acid.
    B. When the electricity is produced from coal-fired power plants.
    C. When the electricity is produced from solar energy or natural gas.
    D. When the batteries can be recharged once before disposal.

28. Which of the following is NOT a reason ozone is the most harmful component of photochemical smog?

    A. Ozone reduces visibility.
    B. Ozone lowers crop yields.
    C. Ozone absorbs ultraviolet radiation.
    D. Ozone causes a variety of health problems.

FILL IN:

1. Smokestacks that have been fitted with electrostatic precipitators, fabric filters, scrubbers, or other technologies remove _____ _____, a common air pollutant.

2. Careful handling of hydrocarbons, such as solvents and petroleum, reduces _____ from spills and evaporation.

3. The most serious indoor air pollutant is likely to be _____ , a colorless, tasteless radioactive gas produced naturally during the radioactive decay of uranium in the earth's crust.

4. _____ (O_3) is a form of oxygen considered a pollutant in one part of the atmosphere but an essential component in another.

5. _____ _____ _____ are emitted, unchanged, from a source directly into the atmosphere.

6. _____ _____ _____ form from chemical reactions involving primary air pollutants.

7. Pollution is worst where _____ _____ is highest.

8. _____ _____ is a brownish orange haze formed by chemical reactions involving sunlight.

9. The _____ extends from 10 to 45 kilometers above the surface of the Earth.

10. Solid particulate matter is generally referred to as _____.

11. Liquid suspensions in the air are commonly called _____.

12. Tropospheric _____ is a secondary air pollutant that forms when sunlight catalyzes a reaction between oxygen, nitrogen oxides, and volatile hydrocarbons.

13. The principal pollutants in _____ _____ are sulfur oxides and particulate matter.

14. Certain types of _____ (surface features) increase the likelihood of thermal inversions.

15. _____ _____ consists of thousands of different solid and liquid particles that are suspended in the atmosphere.

16. Radon and its decay products emit alpha particles, a form of _____ _____ that is very damaging to tissue but cannot penetrate very far into the body.

17. _____ is a colorless, odorless gas that is the principal component of natural gas.

18. Unlike stratospheric ozone, ozone in the _____ -- the layer of atmosphere closest to the Earth's surface-- is a human-made air pollutant.

19. An area of local heat production associated with high population density is known as a(n) _____ .

20. Cities located on the leeward side of mountains, near the coast, or in valleys are prime candidates for _____ _____ .

21. One photochemical reaction occurs among nitrogen oxides, volatile hydrocarbons, and oxygen in the atmosphere to produce ozone; this reaction requires _____ .

22. In the stratosphere, from 2 to 28 miles above the Earth's surface, oxygen reacts with ultraviolet radiation coming from the sun to form _____ _____ .

23. _____ are a diverse group of carbon- and hydrogen-containing compounds that have a wide range of effects on human and animal health.

24. Inside the _____ (the part of the ear that perceives sound) are approximately 24,000 hair cells that detect differences in pressure caused by sound waves.

25. Some consumers may be discouraged from purchasing new automobiles because of the cost increase that is expected to result from installing _____ _____ _____ .

26. Methanol and ethanol are _____ _____ that burn much cleaner than gasoline and can be made from renewable resources such as agricultural waste.

27. Some chemicals enter food webs and become concentrated in the body fat of animals at the top of the food chain, in a process called _____ _____ .

28. Some car designs have _____ _____ that, without flame, combine stored hydrogen with oxygen from the air to produce electricity.

29. The _____ _____ _____ of 1970, 1977, and 1990 have required progressively stricter controls of motor vehicle emissions.

30. The process in which volatile chemicals evaporate from land as far away as the tropics and are transported by winds to higher latitudes, where they condense and fall to the ground is known as the _____ .

31. Relative loudness is expressed numerically using the _____ scale or a modified decibel scale called the decibel-A (dbA) scale, which takes into account high-pitched sounds to which the human ear is more sensitive.

32. The _____ is the layer of atmosphere closest to the Earth's surface.

33. Polluted air in enclosed places such as homes and automobiles is knowns as _____ _____ _____.

34. The word _____ was coined at the beginning of the 20th century for the smoky fog that was so prevalent in London because of coal combustion.

35. The _____ _____ _____ is the presence of air pollution inside office buildings that can cause eye irritations, nausea, headaches, respiratory infections, depression, and fatigue.

36. The _____ is an invisible layer of gases that envelops the Earth.

37. Automobiles and trucks release significant quantities of nitrogen oxides, carbon oxides, particulates, and hydrocarbons as a result of the _____ of gasoline.

38. Urban heat islands affect local air currents and contribute to the buildup of pollutants, especially particulates, with which they form _____ _____ over cities.

39. Sulfur trioxide reacts with water to form another secondary air pollutant, _____ _____.

40. Sulfur can be removed from coal before it is burned by processes like _____ _____.

41. _____ _____ consists of gases, liquids, or solids present in the atmosphere in high enough levels to harm humans, other organisms, or materials.

42. The _____ _____ _____ mandates a 90 percent reduction in the atmospheric emissions of 189 toxic and cancer-causing chemicals by 2003.

43. _____ _____, emitted by cell respiration and combustion, is a colorless, odorless, and tasteless gas that traps heat in the atmosphere and is therefore involved in global climate change.

TRUE OR FALSE:

1. True False Air pollution is involved in acid deposition, global temperature changes, and stratospheric ozone depletion.

2. True False Air pollution is a lesser health threat to children than it is to adults.

3. True False Most particulate matter eventually settles out of the atmosphere, but small particles, some of which are especially harmful to humans, remain suspended in the atmosphere forever.

4. True False Although radon is emitted into the atmosphere, it gets diluted and dispersed and is of little consequence outdoors.

5. True False Air pollutants do not come from natural sources.

6. True False Loud, high-pitched noise injures the hair cells in the cochlea.

7. True False Noise pollution can be reduced by producing less noise.

8. True False The global distillation effect prevents remote arctic regions from becoming contaminated by volatile chemicals.

9. True False Efforts to make our homes more energy-efficient have increased the radon hazard.

10. True False The odor of natural gas comes from sulfur compounds that are deliberately added so that humans can detect the presence of the gas.

11. True False Tropospheric ozone replenishes the ozone that has been depleted from the stratosphere.

12. True False There is direct scientific evidence that links electromagnetic fields to human health problems.

MAKING DECISIONS:

1. You are on a committee for your local hospital. You are trying to raise funds to replace the hospital incinerator with a more expensive state of the art incinerator. Some community members argue that the hospital should not be allowed to burn waste material. Why does a medical facility burn waste instead of sending it to the landfill? What are the environmental problems associated with each option? What compromise can be reached?

2. Examine Figure 19-10: A comparison of 1970 and 1993 emissions in the United States on page 442. You only have enough resources to make further reductions in ONE of the five pollutants listed in the graph. How will you decide which one?

DOING SCIENCE:

1. The following website contains information about a project to study the effects of roofing materials on urban heat islands.

http://EandE.LBL.gov/HeatIsland/

They are testing different materials to use for the roofs of buildings in large urban areas. Their primary concern is to find materials that reflect more sunlight. Before you visit the site, answer the following questions:

What is a heat island?
How does it form?
Why would they be interested in reflective materials for urban roofs?
What do you think a good hypothesis would be for these tests?

Check out their research (or search for the words "urban heat island" using your favorite search engine). Did you come up with a similar hypothesis to theirs?

2. You can create your own version of an electrostatic precipitator. Tear a piece of paper into very small pieces and put them on a pile in front of you. Run a comb through your hair until it makes your hair stand out. Now hold the comb over the pile of papers.

CHECKING WHAT YOU KNOW: (HINT)

MULTIPLE CHOICE: (HINT)

1. D	8. B	15. A	22. C
2. A	9. C	16. C	23. C
3. B	10. A	17. B	24. C
4. A	11. A	18. A	25. C
5. C	12. D	19. C	26. C
6. A	13. D	20. D	27. C
7. A	14. B	21. B	

FILL IN: (HINT)

1. particulate matter
2. air pollution
3. radon
4. Ozone
5. Primary air pollutants
6. Secondary air pollutants
7. population density
8. Photochemical smog
9. stratosphere
10. dust
11. mists
12. ozone
13. industrial smog
14. topography
15. Particulate matter
16. ionizing radiation
17. Methane
18. troposphere
19. urban heat island
20. thermal inversions
21. solar energy
22. ozone
23. Hydrocarbons
24. cochlea
25. pollution control devices
26. alcohol fuels
27. biological magnification
28. fuel cells
29. Clean Air Acts
30. global distillation effect
31. decibel (db)
32. troposphere
33. indoor air pollution
34. smog
35. sick building syndrome
36. atmosphere
37. combustion
38. dust domes
39. sulfuric acid
40. coal gasification
41. Air pollution
42. Clean Air Act
43. Carbon dioxide

TRUE OR FALSE: (HINT)

1. true	4. true	7. false	10. false
2. false	5. false	8. true	11. false
3. false	6. true	9. true	12. false

MAKING DECISIONS: (HINT)

1. Read the Envriobrief "Medical Pollution" on page 443. Waste materials that come in contact with human body fluids must be considered biologically hazardous. Burning the wastes is the best way to ensure that the hazard is eliminated. Materials sent to landfills or disposed of by dumping into the ocean have the possibility of resurfacing and endangering lives. (Many pathogens are able to survive harsh conditions for long periods of time. It is believed, for example, that the curse of the Pharaohs is nothing more than exposure to pathogens surviving in the pyramids for thousands of years.) Disposal of waste in landfills creates the potential for future infections. Disposal of waste in incinerators creates air pollution. Some possible ways to compromise...

- Carefully separate non-hazardous from hazardous waste to reduce the volume that must be incinerated.
- Investigate other sterilization methods.

2. There are several approaches to solving this problem. You may decide based on which pollutant is still emitted in the greatest amount, which has shown the least improvement over time, which one causes the most harm, which one will provide the greatest benefit from a health standpoint, which one will be most cost-effective. It may be that reducing the amount of volatile organics by two metric tons per year will have a greater impact on human health than reducing the amount of carbon monoxide by 30 metric tons per year.

DOING SCIENCE: (HINT)

1. Urban areas typically have temperatures that are 6-8°F higher than the surrounding countryside. These regions of elevated temperatures are called urban heat islands. You have already studied how they can affect the local air conditions and create dust domes. It is this isolating effect that gives rise to the term island.

There are two factors that contribute to the formation of urban heat islands. The first factor is the increased absorption of solar radiation by the dark surfaces in buildings, concrete, and pavement. (You can review solar energy collection in chapter 12 to better understand why these structures store heat.) The second factor is the increase in heat produced by human activity.

The scientists are interested in reflective materials because they believe that if more radiation is reflected away from the urban area, less heat will accumulate there. One hypothesis might be:

If you put reflective material on the roof, the temperature of the building will be lower. Think about what happens when you get into a dark car with dark seats on a hot summer day.

Check out what the scientists are doing and compare it with what you hypothesized.

2. You should observe the papers "jump" toward the comb. This is caused by the negatively charged comb attracting the positively charged papers. Humidity and other local conditions may affect your results.

CHAPTER 20 -- GLOBAL ATMOSPHERIC CHANGES

LEARNING THE LANGUAGE:

acid deposition
acidic
aerosol
aerosol effect
agroforestry
air pollution
alkaline
carbon dioxide
carbon "sink"
chlorofluorocarbons (CFCs)
circumpolar vortex
clean-coal technologies
climate
combustion
deltas (river)
dry deposition
endangered species
energy efficiency
evaporation
forest decline

global warming
greenhouse effect
greenhouse gas
infrared radiation
iron hypothesis
methane
Montreal Protocol
nitrogen oxide
oxygen
ozone
"ozone hole"
pH
photosynthesis
phytoplankton
soil chemistry
sulfur haze
sulfur oxide
ultraviolet radiation
wet deposition
zooplankton

CHECKING WHAT YOU KNOW:

MULTIPLE CHOICE:

1. The graph below is a representation of the average temperature data for the past hundred years. The Y-axis represents increasing temperature. The X-axis is time in years. The line labeled LOW is the lowest estimates of temperature increase. The line labeled HIGH represents the highest estimates of global temperature change. (The estimates come from global climate change models that make differing assumptions about greenhouse gas emissions and their effects.) Which of the following statements is NOT true about this graph?

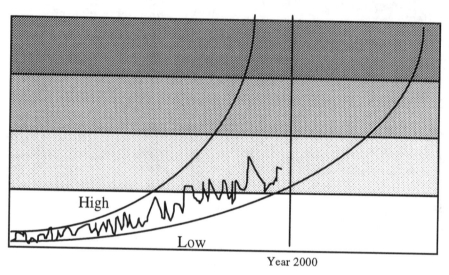

Year 2000

    A. This graph includes real climate data. (The zigzag line between the arcs.)
    B. This graph colors higher temperatures darker so that they look more ominous.
    C. This graph estimates what will happen to global temperature beyond the data that are currently available.
    D. This graph is an accurate projection of global climate change over the next fifty years.

2. Which of the following is NOT a likely result of increasing the size of the hole in the ozone over the Antarctic?

    A. The number of skin cancers is likely to increase.
    B. Polar bears will go blind.
    C. Corals and ocean living organisms will be damaged by increasing amounts of ultraviolet radiation.
    D. The amount of ultraviolet radiation reaching the surface of the planet will increase.

3. Which of the following is NOT a likely consequence of heating the atmosphere?

A. A shift in the geographical range of species.
B. Some areas will receive more rain than they used to.
C. Flooding of river deltas will cause a loss of fertile land for food production.
D. More ultraviolet radiation will reach the surface of the planet.

4. A serious regional problem caused by sulfur and nitrogen oxides is

A. global warming
B. thinning ozone

C. acid deposition
D. CFC production

5. The Montreal Protocol was signed in 1987. It attempts to ban the production and use of _____, which cause ozone depletion.

A. chlorine   B. lead   C. DDT   D. CFCs

6. Which of the following arguments about the hole in the ozone is NOT based on a FACT?

A. The ozone hole allows higher levels of UV radiation to reach the surface.
B. Volcanoes spew sulfur and chlorine compounds into the atmosphere, but they probably cannot reach the stratosphere.
C. There is no documentation linking CFCs to ozone depletion.
D. Humans are responsible for the hole in the ozone because breakdown products of CFCs have been found in the stratosphere.

7. Which of the following stores carbon away from the carbon cycle for millions of years?

A. trees
B. carbon dioxide

C. ocean phytoplankton
D. fossil fuels

8. Which of the following statements BEST describes the greenhouse effect?

A. Carbon dioxide and other greenhouse gases bounce heat back to the surface of the planet rather than allowing it to escape into space.
B. Solar energy entering the atmosphere is bounced back out to space by greenhouse gases.
C. The hole in the ozone allows more ultraviolet radiation to reach the surface of the planet.
D. Aerosols cool the planet by reflecting sunlight away from the Earth.

9. The air conditioner in your 1987 Dodge Omni is broken. You take it to your auto repair shop and learn that the cost of replacement is going to be more than the car is worth. While talking to the mechanic, you learn that most of this cost is caused by the ban on CFCs. While doing some more research, you learn that this ban was instituted by Congress as a response to the reports of the hole in the ozone. Before writing to your congressman you need to learn more about the issue. Which of the following sources would be the most reliable and least biased?

A. An *Autoweek* editorial on the poor quality of substitute molecules.
B. A local newspaper article on the hole in the ozone.
C. An article in *Science* by a group measuring the effect of CFCs in the upper atmosphere.
D. An advertisement in the *National Inquirer*.

10. The reason a hole in the ozone is of concern is because

A. Ultraviolet radiation that reaches the surface of the planet can damage DNA.
B. Ozone reacts with chlorine to form ClO.
C. Ozone is an air pollutant, and if it isn't in the upper atmosphere it has to be in the troposphere causing problems for endangered species.
D. Ozone is formed when electrical motors burn up.

11. Which of the following mechanisms causes the ocean to rise without actually adding more water to it?

A. thermal expansion
B. melting polar ice caps
C. changes in precipitation
D. thawing of glaciers

12. "CFC production increased to 1.1 million tons annually by 1985, unleashing the potential to destroy 20% of the ozone layer over North America." Which part of this statement is a fact?

A. CFC production directly correlates with the amount of ozone destroyed over the site of production.
B. 1.1 million tons of CFCs can destroy 20% of the ozone.
C. The ozone shield gets destroyed by CFCs over North America.
D. CFC production was 1.1 million tons in 1985.

13. Which of the following is NOT a greenhouse gas?

A. sulfur haze
B. carbon dioxide
C. methane
D. tropospheric ozone

14. Which of the following things will NOT reduce emissions of greenhouse gases?

A. Eat more meat.
B. Reduce dependence on fossil fuels.
C. Plant more trees.
D. Encourage growth of producers such as phytoplankton in the world's oceans.

15. The aerosol effect causes

A. global warming.
B. atmospheric cooling.

C. ozone depletion.
D. acid deposition.

16. The hole in the ozone is thought to be caused by a reaction between ozone and

_____.

A. ultraviolet radiation
B. carbon dioxide

C. NO$_2$
D. chorine or bromine

17. Acid rain has a pH of

A. 3 - 4   B. 5 - 6   C. 7 - 8   D. 10 - 14

18. Examine the data in the following graph, which shows the amount of ozone over the Antarctic over the last 40 years. Can you believe this data without question? Why?

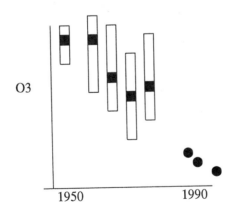

O3

1950   1990

A. Yes. Data have been collected by scientists in the Antarctic for over 40 years, and it clearly represents a decline in the amount of ozone. Scientists would not report data that was untrue.
B. Yes. If you draw a line between the points, you see that ozone has been decreasing for the last 40 years.

C. No. The data were collected by people who want to ban all useful chemicals, and so it is biased. No one who has an opinion about an issue can collect data that is useful.

D. No. It is curious that the style of the points has changed and that the points change where there is the most dramatic drop in ozone. I would want to know more about why the points are different on this graph before I absolutely accepted the data.

19. A greenhouse gas is thought to heat up the atmosphere by

A. Scattering incoming solar radiation.
B. Causing exothermic chemical reactions in the stratosphere.
C. Reflecting heat back to the surface of the planet.
D. Helping more plants to grow in temperate regions in the winter.

20. The surfaces of soil particles are _____ charged, and in acidified soil, hydrogen ions from acid deposition are attracted to the soil particles, displacing ions such as calcium and magnesium.

A. negatively   B. positively   C. neutrally

21. The following equations represent the natural formation and decay of what molecule?

```
O + O₂ ---> O₃
```

```
O₃ + ultraviolet radiation ---> O + O₂
```

A. PCBs   C. photochemical smog
B. ozone   D. sulfur haze

22. The increase in global temperature observed since the 1940s is caused by humans releasing greater and greater amounts of greenhouse gases such as carbon dioxide.

A. This statement is TRUE. It is proven by the data.
B. This statement is FALSE. It is disproven by looking at changes in global temperature using a geologic time scale.
C. The data appear to support this statement, but we do not really know whether this statement is true or false.

23. If the carbon dioxide levels increased enough to cause a global temperature increase of 3°C, which of the following species would be most likely to see an increase in habitat range?

A. polar bear   C. alpine spruces
B. malaria parasite   D. Minke whales

24. Which of the following processes removes carbon dioxide from the atmosphere?

    A. photosynthesis
    B. respiration
    C. combustion
    D. decomposition

25. Which of the following methods is NOT likely to slow global warming?

    A. Plant trees
    B. Ban the use of CFCs (chlorofluorocarbons).
    C. Increase sulfur emissions substantially to general sulfur haze.
    D. Encourage the growth of marine phytoplankton by seeding the oceans with nutrients.

26. Examine the graph in figure 20-6. What is represented by the horizontal line at zero?

    A. Zero degrees Celsius.
    B. The average global temperature in 1960.
    C. The average global temperature for the years 1960-1995.
    D. Global warming in the last twenty years.

FILL IN:

1. _____ _____ causes the pH of surface water and soil to decrease.

2. This type of acid deposition, which consists of sulfuric acid and nitric acids in precipitation, is sometimes called _____ _____ .

3. Dry, sulfuric and nitric acid-containing particles that settle out of the air are sometimes called _____ _____ .

4. Several studies found that birds living in areas with pronounced _____ _____ were much more likely to lay eggs with thin, fragile shells that break or dry out before the chicks hatch.

5. In the summer of 1991 the fritillary was listed as a(n) _____ _____, but this federal protection will not keep it from becoming extinct if the climate continues to warm.

6. Some experts predict that _____ _____ will cause tropical and subtropical regions, where many of the world's poorest people live, to be hardest hit by declining agricultural productivity.

7. Global warming will probably cause greater _____ from the Earth's surface, resulting in more clouds.

8. Many trees that are not dead are exhibiting symptoms of _____ _____, which is characterized by gradual deterioration and often death of trees.

9. The use by consumers of smuggled _____ discourages them from switching to alternatives and, more importantly, increases the damage to the ozone layer.

10. Carbon dioxide and certain other atmospheric pollutants trap solar heat in the atmosphere and may cause the Earth's _____ to warm.

11. A pH of 7 is neither acidic nor alkaline, whereas a pH less than 7 indicates a(n) _____ solution.

12. Increasing the _____ _____ of automobiles and appliances reduces the output of carbon dioxide and helps mitigate global warming.

13. The _____ _____ is a mass of cold air that circulates around the southern polar region, in effect isolating it from the warmer air in the rest of the world.

14. Many scientists are convinced that ecosystems will not recover from acid rain damage until substantial reductions in _____ _____ emissions occur.

15. Developed nations may adopt carbon and energy taxes to help reduce their _____ _____ emissions.

16. Carbon dioxide emissions from the _____ of fossil fuels cause the air to retain heat.

17. It appears that northern forests may have acted as a _____ _____ by using increased inputs of carbon dioxide for accelerated growth.

18. When the _____ _____ breaks up each year, the ozone-depleted air spreads northward, diluting ozone levels in the stratosphere over South America, New Zealand, and Australia.

19. Installation of scrubbers in the smokestacks of coal-fired power plants and use of _____ _____ _____ to burn coal without excessive emissions effectively diminish acid deposition.

20. The concentration of atmospheric _____ _____ has increased from about 280 parts per million approximately 200 years ago (before the Industrial Revolution began) to 361 parts per million in 1995.

21. The countries that are most vulnerable to a rise in sea level have dense populations in low-lying river _____.

22. _____ uses both forestry and agricultural techniques to improve degraded areas.

23. Acid deposition may contribute to forest decline by changing _____ _____.

24. _____ (O_3) is a form of oxygen that is a human-made pollutant in the troposphere but a naturally produced, essential component in the stratosphere.

25. Carbon dioxide and certain other atmospheric pollutants trap solar heat in the atmosphere, a phenomenon known as the _____ _____.

26. _____ and other chlorine-containing compounds slowly drift up to the stratosphere, where UV radiation breaks them down, releasing chlorine.

27. Atmospheric carbon dioxide is removed from the air by growing forests, which incorporate the carbon into leaves, stems, and roots through the process of _____.

28. Certain areas of the ocean are rich in nutrients such as nitrogen but very low in iron; these areas also have very few _____ (microscopic algae).

29. The _____ _____ was tested in 1995 when small amounts of dissolved iron were added to an area of the Pacific Ocean.

30. _____ _____ is heat.

31. The buildup of carbon dioxide and other greenhouse gases causes the _____ _____, which results in global warming.

32. The stratosphere contains a layer of _____ that shields the surface from much of the ultraviolet radiation coming from the sun.

33. Some of the possible effects of increased _____ _____ penetration in water are to disrupt photosynthesis in algae and aquatic plants and to cause sunburn damage in fish.

34. The _____ _____ that was discovered over Antarctica occurs annually between September and November.

35. _____, which come from both natural and human sources, are tiny particles that are so small that they remain suspended in the atmosphere for days, weeks, or even months.

36. Under certain conditions found in the stratosphere, chlorine or bromine is capable of attacking ozone and converting it into _____.

37. The atmospheric cooling that occurs where aerosol pollution is greatest is known as the _____ _____.

38. _____ _____, the aerosol that causes acid deposition, also cools the planet by reflecting sunlight away from the earth.

TRUE OR FALSE:

1. True False Developing and adopting strategies to adapt to climate change implies an assumption that global warming is avoidable.

2. True False A report published by the National Academy of Sciences concluded that global warming is responsible for the decline of fishes in lakes of the Adirondack Mountains and in Nova Scotia rivers.

3. True False Scientists agree over the future rate and magnitude of climate change as well as what regional patterns may emerge.

4. True False Acid deposition correlates well with areas that are experiencing tree damage.

5. True False Developing countries will likely resist pressure from developed nations to decrease fossil fuel consumption.

6. True False Purchase and use of aerosol antiperspirants in the United States today causes the release of harmful CFCs.

7. True False Nitrogen oxide emissions are harder to control than sulfur dioxide emissions because nitrogen oxides come mainly from automobiles.

8. True False The development of alternatives to fossil fuels offers a solution to the challenge of global warming caused by carbon dioxide.

9. True False A single chlorine or bromine atom can breakdown many thousands of ozone molecules.

10. True False Pollution abatement issues are quite complex within one country, but are magnified even more in international disputes.

11.   True   False   Today all foam packaging made in the United States is ozone-friendly.

12.   True   False   Human-produced pollution is the only cause of ozone depletion.

13.   True   False   The atmospheric warming that occurs where aerosol pollution is greatest is known as the aerosol effect.

14.   True   False   UV radiation penetrates into lake waters as a result of climate warming.

PEOPLE WHO MATTER:

1. Molina, Rowland, and Crutzen were awarded the 1995 Nobel prize in chemistry. The following website provides more information about Mario Molina. It also contains links to similar information about Sherwood Rowland and Paul Crutzen.

       http://nobel.eb.com/nobel/micro/721_70.html

Open this location or plug the three men's names into your search engine. What did they do to earn this prestigious award? Why is this significant?

MAKING CONNECTIONS:

1. Some people argue that a mechanism for putting more carbon dioxide into long term storage already exists. They cite the lack of decay of organic material stored as solid waste in landfills. Paper and garbage stored in these sites do not readily decompose. If this material is composted, the carbon is released into the atmosphere. Analyze this position. What are the benefits of such long-term storage? What are the environmental consequences?

2. Explain why the latitude 65°S has a greater average increase in ultraviolet radiation exposure than 65°N.

MAKING DECISIONS:

1. By the time you read this book, the United Nations Framework Convention on Climate Change in Kyoto, Japan (December 1997) will already have taken place. One of the purposes of this meeting is to establish binding limits to the emissions of greenhouse gases. The countries that will be affected the most are the developed nations because they have the greatest per capita emissions. Developing nations will not be asked to meet the same standards. What are the arguments for and against this disparity of outcomes? What

actually happened at and as a result of the convention? Do you think your country or your life will be changed in ten years as a result of this convention? If so, how?

CHECKING WHAT YOU KNOW: (HINT)

MULTIPLE CHOICE: (HINT)

1. D	8. A	15. B	22. C
2. B	9. C	16. D	23. B
3. D	10. A	17. A	24. A
4. C	11. A	18. D	25. C
5. D	12. D	19. C	26. C
6. A	13. A	20. A	
7. D	14. A	21. B	

FILL IN: (HINT)

1. Acid deposition
2. wet deposition
3. dry deposition
4. acid deposition
5. endangered species
6. global warming
7. evaporation
8. forest decline
9. Chlorofluorocarbons (CFCs)
10. climate
11. acidic
12. energy efficiency
13. circumpolar vortex
14. nitrogen oxide
15. carbon dioxide
16. combustion
17. carbon "sink"
18. circumpolar vortex
19. clean-coal technologies
20. carbon dioxide
21. deltas
22. Agroforestry
23. soil chemistry
24. Ozone
25. greenhouse effect
26. Chlorofluorocarbons (CFCs)
27. photosynthesis
28. phytoplankton
29. iron hypothesis
30. Infrared radiation
31. greenhouse effect
32. ozone
33. ultraviolet radiation
34. "ozone hole"
35. Aerosols
36. oxygen
37. aerosol effect
38. Sulfur haze

TRUE OR FALSE: (HINT)

1. false	5. true	9. true	13. false
2. false	6. false	10. true	14. true
3. false	7. true	11. true	
4. true	8. true	12. false	

PEOPLE WHO MATTER: (HINT)

1. Molina, Rowland, and Crutzen won the prize for explaining the chemistry of ozone depletion. In 1970, Crutzen reported that nitrous oxide is capable of splitting ozone. Four years later, Molina and Rowland described similar atmospheric chemistry for CFCs. Neither Crutzen's nor Molina and Rowland's research was universally accepted although Crutzen's work did make it easier for the following group. CFCs were considered to be inert chemicals with no environmental effects nor with any human health concerns. The work of Molina and Rowland caused a major change in the chemical industry. All non-essential or easily replaced CFC functions were banned. A major effort to find alternatives has been launched and has been fairly successful.

Although these men published their original results in the early seventies, it was not until the mid-nineties that they were recognized. In the intervening years, the hole in the ozone was discovered and breakdown products of CFCs were found in the stratosphere over Antarctica. These events helped to confirm the original results and convince much of the scientific community that the laboratory results could happen in the stratosphere.

MAKING CONNECTIONS: (HINT)

1. The basic argument here is that carbon can be stored in landfills for long periods of time. The benefit is that carbon stored here is not contributing to global warming. The problem with this is that landfills create their own environmental problems; they are land-intensive, cause habitat destruction, concentrate toxins, and allow contaminants to leach into groundwater.

2. The largest hole in the ozone occurs over the South Pole where the formation of the stratospheric clouds and the circumpolar vortex create conditions that facilitate ozone destruction. These conditions do not appear to occur to the same extent over the North Pole, although some thinning of the ozone has been reported there.

MAKING DECISIONS: (HINT)
1.
- For: Developed nations use most of the resources and have the highest per capita emissions of greenhouse gasses. Therefore it is reasonable to expect them to make the greatest changes.

- Against: The people in developing nations would like to have the same lifestyle as people in developed nations. The only way they can accomplish this is to consume more which must lead to greater emissions. If they are not held to the same standards as developed nations, the reduction in emissions by developed nations will be outweighed by the increase in emissions by developing nations.

- *Against: Not holding developing nations to the same emissions standards may give them a competitive economic edge.*

- *Another factor to consider: Developed nations should provide developing nations with the resources and technology to limit emissions.*

CHAPTER 21 -- WATER AND SOIL POLLUTION

LEARNING THE LANGUAGE:

anaerobic digestion
artificial eutrophication
biological oxygen demand (BOD)
bioremediation
capillary movement
chlorine
coliform bacteria
combined sewer overflow
combined sewer system
dilution
disease-causing organisms
enrichment
eutrophication
fecal coliform test
Great Lakes Toxic Substance Control
        Agreement
groundwater
hydrocarbons
hypoxia
inorganic plant and algal nutrients
inorganic chemicals
irrigation
limiting factor
maximum contaminant level
nonpoint source pollution
oligotrophic
organic compounds

petroleum
phytoremediation
point source pollution
polluted runoff
primary treatment
radiation
radon
Refuse Act of 1899
reservoir
Resource, Conservation, and Recovery Act
        of 1976
runoff
salinization
salt marsh
secondary treatment
sediment pollution
selenium
sewage
sewage sludge
surface water
tertiary treatment
thermal pollution
trickling filters
ultraviolet radiation
urban runoff
vapor extraction
watershed

CHECKING WHAT YOU KNOW:

MULTIPLE CHOICE:

1. What is/are a source of BOD found in the Ganges River in India, but not commonly found in other rivers?

    A. lack of sewage treatment
    B. the millions of people living along the river
    C. dumping of industrial water into the river
    D. human corpses

2. The Great Lake that is least polluted is?

    A. Michigan   B. Ontario   C. Erie   D. Superior

3. Your town is planning to open a new water treatment plant on a local river to provide drinking water. You need to identify potential sources of pollution. Which of the following would NOT be a cause for concern?

    A. Agricultural fields adjacent to the river
    B. An old landfill close to the river
    C. An aquifer underneath the river
    D. Clearcutting in the hills around the river

4. In salinized soil, water moves _____ plant cells.

    A. into
    B. out of
    C. neither into nor out of

5. Two sportsmen were riding snowmobiles on the Saginaw Bay of Lake Michigan in January. They were near a nuclear power plant. They accidentally drove into a patch of water not covered by ice. This open water was caused by _____ from the power plant.

    A. salinization   C. thermal pollution
    B. radioactivity   D. eutrophication

6. D.O. is defined as

    A. Dead On Arrival
    B. The concentration of oxygen necessary for life.
    C. The concentration of oxygen dissolved in water.
    D. The concentration of oxygen used by decomposers.

7. It is _____ to remove salts from salinized soils.

    A. extremely easy   C. relatively hard
    B. relatively simple   D. extremely difficult

8. Why is it NOT advisable to put a septic tank in close proximity to a freshwater well?

   A. Are you kidding? You always put the well and septic system within 10 feet of each other to make sure that the well doesn't run dry.

   B. Federal regulations specify that in order to keep small well drilling operators in business, you must drill two holes. Otherwise, you would have one well/septic system.

   C. It reduces the distance between the waste water and the aquifer, thereby reducing the amount of filtration and increasing the risk of contamination.

   D. It would slow down the recharge process and you wouldn't get as much fresh water.

9. Under normal conditions, soil water moves _____ plant root cells.

   A. into

   B. out of

   C. neither into nor out of

10. Petroleum may be a contaminant in groundwater. The origin of the petroleum typically is

   A. accidents involving tankers

   B. overflow of automobile fuel tanks

   C. refineries illegally dumping petroleum products

   D. leaking underground storage tanks

11. In June after fish started dying and the river started smelling bad, the City of Toledo pumped water out of the Ottowa River and then sprayed it back. The reason they did this was because:

   A. they were trying to disperse the smell faster.

   B. the river had a high BOD, which caused the oxygen level to drop and the fish to die; they thought that adding air (i.e. oxygen) into the water would help.

   C. children wanted to play in the river, and increasing the oxygen made it safer.

   D. the pumps filtered out all of the toxic chemicals in the river and allowed the fish to live; the fish eat algae and purify the river.

12. Which of the following diseases is NOT waterborne?

   A. typhoid   B. AIDS   C. cholera   D. polio

13. You go to your usual gas station on the corner to fill up your tank. Instead of seeing gas pumps and a cashier's booth, you see a big hole and piles of dirt. You ask one of the workers what is going on and he tells you that the EPA has required the station to replace all of the underground storage tanks with newer tanks that have double walls. The EPA has required this because:

    A. it is very costly to replace tanks and to haul the potentially contaminated soil underneath to a toxic waste dump.
    B. leaking underground storage tanks are one of the biggest sources of petroleum contamination in groundwater supplies.
    C. the EPA likes to make sure that the soil under gas stations and factories is aerated at least once every 10 years.
    D. the underground storage tanks are made of CFCs that can damage the ozone.

14. Which of the following contaminants is NOT found in water after primary and secondary treatments?

    A. dissolved minerals   C. silt
    B. heavy metals   D. viruses

15. The most immediate threat to human health caused by water pollution is

    A. waterborne diseases that cause dysentery.
    B. toxic chemicals such as lead.
    C. bioaccumulating chemicals such as DDT and dioxin.
    D. carcinogens such as PCBs.

16. Martin had to build an artificial hill on his wetland farm in order to comply with health and safety regulations when he installed his new septic system and drain field. This hill:

    A. maintain the proper distance between the sewage and the water table to prevent groundwater contamination.
    B. creates a high spot for observing weather events.
    C. avoids subsidence caused by groundwater depletion.
    D. saves money because building over a swamp is more cost effective that building in it.

17. Which of the following is NOT one of the federal laws that have the most impact on water quality today?

    A. The Environmental Protection Act   C. The Clean Water Act
    B. The Safe Drinking Water Act   D. The Water Quality Act

18. Inorganic plant and algal nutrients

    A. cause a reduction in photosynthesis because they increase turbidity.
    B. cause the excessive growth of algae and aquatic plants.
    C. indicate the presence of pathogens.
    D. are a common problem in irrigated arid and semiarid lands.

19. Which of the following is NOT true of the cleanup of contaminated groundwater?

    A. It is costly.
    B. It takes years.
    C. It is not always technically feasible.
    D. It is simple.

20. Which of the following is NOT a major source of human-induced water pollution?

    A. agriculture runoff
    B. sewage
    C. industrial waste
    D. fossil fuel combustion

21. Under normal conditions, the water concentration inside plant cells is _____ the water concentration in the soil.

    A. lower than
    B. the same as
    C. greater than

22. Which water pollutant enters the water supply through old pipes and solder in public water distribution systems, homes and other buildings?

    A. Chlorinated solvents
    B. Pathogenic bacteria
    C. Lead
    D. PCB's

23. The maximum permissible amount in drinking water of any water pollutant that might adversely affect human health:

    A. law of tolerance
    B. limiting factor
    C. national emission limits
    D. maximum contaminant level

24. The use of bacteria and other microorganisms to degrade organic toxins in contaminated soil.

    A. Dilution
    B. Vapor extraction
    C. Bioremediation
    D. Phytoremediation

25. Lake Erie was declared dead in the 1960s as a result of increased use of phosphorus-containing fertilizers and detergents. The resulting algal blooms and fish kills were an example of:

A. groundwater contamination
B. artificial eutrophication

C. dead zone
D. thermal pollution

26. Fish started dying in the Ottawa river in Toledo because a company was dumping organic wastes into the river. River flow was greatly reduced at the time because there had not been much rain. The organic waste caused the fish to die because

A. all organic molecules are toxic.
B. the organic waste created BOD which depleted the oxygen content of the water.
C. the organic waste created BOD which depleted the carbon dioxide content of the water.
D. the organic waste made the water too thick for the fish to swim.

27. The technician at the your water treatment plant measured high levels of coliform bacteria. She immediately notified her supervisor, who started treating the water with increased levels of chlorine. Why was this action taken?

A. coliform bacteria are found in the intestines of humans and other animals.
B. coliform bacteria produce ozone, and chlorine eliminates it.
C. an increase in coliform bacteria indicates an increase in the amount of fecal material, which could also contain pathogens.
D. coliform bacteria require chlorine to grow.

29. Groundwater pollution is harder to address than pollution of surface water because

A. in order to purify groundwater, you must first pump it out of the ground. You cannot access it directly like you could a surface stream.
B. groundwater moves slowly, and dilution of groundwater pollutants is a much slower process.
C. it is harder to locate the source and harder to track the flow of groundwater contamination because you have to dig wells.
D. All of these answers describe reasons why groundwater pollution is harder to treat than pollution in surface water.

29. The pond next to a feedlot contains an increased amount of nitrogen and phosphorus, which has caused:

A. fluoridation

B. salinization

C. oligotrophication

D. eutrophication

30. Joshua fishes in a pristine trout stream in Northern Michigan. The last time he was there, the stream was muddy brown and he couldn't see the bottom, let alone any trout. When he explored upstream he found four sites that could have caused this increase in sediment in the river. Which one is the most likely cause?

A. a managed logging operation.

B. an old overgrown cherry orchard.

C. an area covered with new grass and pioneer species that had been the site of a forest fire last year.

D. a construction site where a new cabin is being built

31. Downstream from a sewage treatment discharge point, a river could be characterized by an area of

A. enhanced levels of persistent chemicals.

B. reduced dissolved oxygen concentration.

C. elevated levels of soil sediments.

D. concentrated heavy metals.

FILL IN:

1. _____, such as nitrogen and phosphorus, come from animal wastes and plant residues as well as fertilizer runoff.

2. Soil erosion from fields and rangelands causes _____ _____ in waterways.

3. The _____ deals with the storage and disposal of hazardous wastes and helps prevent groundwater contamination.

4. In _____ _____ sewage sludge is placed in large circular digesters and kept warm to allow anaerobic bacteria to breakdown the organic material.

5. _____ is the enrichment of water by nutrients.

6. Nonpoint source pollution, also called _____ _____, comes from the land rather than from a single point of entry.

7. The use of bacteria and other microorganisms to clean up soil and water pollution is known as _____.

8. _____ is a common problem in irrigated arid and semiarid regions that makes soil unfit for growing most crops.

9. _____ _____ occurs when heated water is released into waterways.

10. The _____ _____ _____ is used to indicate the likely presence of disease-causing agents in water.

11. The amount of oxygen needed by microorganisms to decompose the wastes is called the _____ _____ _____.

12. _____ _____ of sewage removes suspended and floating particles, such as sand and silt, by mechanical processes such as screening and gravitational settling.

13. _____ is the presence of low oxygen levels in coastal waters and it occurs when algae grow rapidly due to the presence of nutrients in the water.

14. _____ _____ is the biological degradation by microorganisms of suspended organic matter in wastewater.

15. The removal of special contaminants such as organic chemicals, nitrogen, and phosphorus from wastewater is called _____ _____.

16. _____ is a naturally occurring radioactive gas that can enter groundwater.

17. Anaerobic digestion, application to soil as a fertilizer, incineration, ocean dumping, and disposal in a sanitary landfill are five possible ways to handle _____ _____.

18. The use of plants to clean up polluted soil, known as _____, is a relatively inexpensive soil-remediation technique, although it requires several to many years before the soil is clean.

19. The United States has attempted to control water pollution through legislation since the passage of the _____, which was intended to reduce the release of pollutants into navigable rivers.

20. _____ _____ _____, such as the organisms that cause typhoid and cholera, may be present in water; they come from the wastes of infected individuals.

21. _____ include such contaminants as the heavy metals mercury and lead.

22. Artificial lakes called _____ are often produced by building a dam across a river or stream.

23. Most strains of _____ do not cause disease, yet they may indicate the presence of pathogens in water.

24. _____ _____ _____, also called polluted runoff, is caused by land pollutants that enter bodies of water over large areas rather than at a single point.

25. In _____ _____, air is injected into or pumped through soil to remove organic compounds that are volatile (evaporate quickly).

26. _____ is discharged into the environment through pipes, sewers, or ditches from specific sites such as factories or sewage treatment plants.

27. _____ is an extremely toxic natural element found in many western soils that causes death and deformity in thousands of migratory birds and other organisms annually.

28. People used to think that the underlying soil and rock through which surface water must seep in order to become _____ , filtered out any contaminants.

29. In the final purification step, drinking water is disinfected by adding _____ to kill any remaining disease-causing agents.

30. When irrigated soil becomes waterlogged, salts may be carried by _____ _____ from groundwater to the soil surface, where they are deposited as a crust of salt.

31. High _____ occurs when the excessive numbers of algae die and are decomposed by bacteria.

32. The _____ is designed to reduce pollution in the Great Lakes by developing coordinated programs among the eight states and two Canadian provinces that border the lakes' ecosystem.

33. _____ _____, most of which are synthetic, are often toxic to aquatic organisms and often persist in the environment for a long time.

34. One of the several types of secondary treatment is _____ _____, in which wastewater trickles through aerated rock beds that contain bacteria and other microorganisms, which degrade the organic material in the water.

35. In one type of secondary treatment, water is aerated and circulated through bacteria-rich particles and then allowed to settle out, forming _____ _____, a slimy mixture of bacteria-laden solids.

36. Many cities have a _____ _____ _____ in which human and industrial wastes are mixed with urban runoff from storm sewers before flowing into the sewage treatment plant.

37. _____ from agricultural and residential land is a major contributor of inorganic plant and algal nutrients such as nitrogen and phosphorus to water.

38. When too much water enters a combined sewer system, the excess, known as _____ _____ _____, flows into nearby waterways without being treated.

39. _____ _____ causes problems by reducing light penetration, covering aquatic organisms, bringing insoluble toxic pollutants into the water, and filling in waterways.

40. _____ is wastewater carried off by drains or sewers (from toilets, washing machines, and showers) and includes water that contains human wastes, soaps, and detergents.

41. Although sewage is the main pollutant produced by cities and towns, municipal waste pollution also has a nonpoint source: _____ _____ from storm sewers.

42. A(n) _____ lake has clear water and supports small populations of aquatic organisms.

43. _____ _____ are synthetic chemicals that are produced by human activities; these include pesticides, solvents, industrial chemicals, and plastics.

44. _____ _____ is a fast, human-induced process that results from the enrichment of water by inorganic plant and algal nutrients.

45. _____ involves running large quantities of water through contaminated soil in order to leach out pollutants such as excess salt.

TRUE OR FALSE:

1. True False When sediments build up to the point where they envelop coral reefs and shellfish beds, they can clog the gills and feeding structures of many aquatic animals.

2. True False Disease-causing agents can be transported into water via sediments.

3. True False The National Research Council announced that properly treated sewage sludge should not be used to fertilize food crops.

4. True False Infectious diseases are expanding worldwide because many people do not have water clean enough to drink or even bathe in.

5. True False Oxygen has an unlimited ability to dissolve in water.

6. True False Turbid water increases the ability of aquatic producers to photosynthesize.

7. True False There may be subtle changes in the activities and behavior of aquatic organisms in thermally polluted water, because temperature affects reproductive cycles, digestion rates, and respiration rates.

8. True False More than 40 years of research have consistently linked fluoridation to cancer, kidney disease, and birth defects.

9. True False Under normal conditions, the dissolved materials in plant cells give them a higher concentration of water than that in soil.

10. True False Dry cell batteries, like those that power portable stereos and flashlights, are by far the greatest source of mercury and cadmium pollution.

11. True False Phosphorus is often the limiting factor in freshwater lakes.

12. True False Most strains of coliform bacteria cause disease in humans.

13. True False The possibility of sea lamprey control is more promising since the recent development of a chemical that sterilizes male sea lampreys.

14. True False Tertiary treatment does little to eliminate dissolved minerals, heavy metals and organic compounds that remain suspended in the wastewater following secondary treatment.

15. True   False   Currently, most of the groundwater supplies in the United States are of good quality.

16. True   False   Soil pollution is important not only in its own right but because so many soil pollutants tend to get into surface water, groundwater, and air.

17. True   False   Soil erosion is a major cause of point source pollution.

18. True   False   Over vast periods of time, oligotrophic lakes and slow-moving streams and rivers become eutrophic naturally.

19. True   False   The water supply for a town is often stored in a reservoir.

20. True   False   Water that has undergone primary and secondary treatment is clear and free of organic wastes such as sewage.

21. True   False   Groundwater pollution, which is caused primarily by soil erosion, increases water turbidity, thereby reducing the photosynthetic productivity of the water.

MAKING CONNECTIONS:

1. Why are recreational boaters going to have to comply with new laws that regulate air and water pollution?

2. Why are soil and water pollution discussed in the same chapter?

3. What is the reason that hand pumps solved the problem of transmission of waterborne illnesses in Kwale, Kenya?

4. Why is heated water considered a form of pollution? Shouldn't fish survive better if the water stays warm and does not get covered with ice in the winter?

MAKING DECISIONS:

1. You live in the middle of a large agricultural region. Your local community is in need of a new wastewater treatment facility. A local group of environmentalists would like the facility to include a tertiary treatment facility. The mayor and several members of the city council are opposed to the additional cost of such a facility. Prepare a speech that explains primary, secondary, and tertiary treatments. Include why tertiary treatment will be of value for your community.

2. Explain the chlorine dilemma. What do you think?

DOING SCIENCE:

1. You discover that a well in your county is contaminated with a unique organic molecule. The actual health effects of this molecule are not known, but since it closely resembles the structure of a known carcinogen, you believe it has the potential to cause problems. How will you determine if this molecule is moving through the groundwater?

CHECKING WHAT YOU KNOW: (HINT)

MULTIPLE CHOICE: (HINT)

1. D	9. A	17. A	25. B
2. D	10. D	18. B	26. B
3. C	11. B	19. D	27. C
4. B	12. B	20. D	28. D
5. C	13. B	21. A	29. D
6. C	14. C	22. C	30. D
7. D	15. A	23. D	31. B
8. C	16. A	24. C	

FILL IN: (HINT)

1. Inorganic plant and algal nutrients
2. sediment pollution
3. Resource, Conservation, and Recovery Act of 1976
4. anaerobic digestion
5. Eutrophication
6. polluted runoff
7. bioremediation
8. Salinization
9. Thermal pollution
10. fecal coliform test
11. biological oxygen demand (BOD)
12. Primary treatment
13. Hypoxia
14. Secondary treatment
15. tertiary treatment
16. Radon
17. sewage sludge
18. phytoremediation
19. Refuse Act of 1899
20. Disease-causing agents
21. Inorganic chemicals
22. reservoirs
23. coliform bacteria
24. Nonpoint source pollution
25. vapor extraction
26. Point source pollution
27. Selenium
28. groundwater
29. chlorine
30. capillary movement
31. BOD (biological oxygen demand)
32. Great Lakes Toxic Substance Control Agreement
33. Organic compounds
34. trickling filters
35. sewage sludge
36. combined sewer system
37. Runoff
38. combined sewer overflow
39. Sediment pollution
40. sewage
41. urban runoff
42. oligotrophic
43. Organic compounds
44. Artificial eutrophication
45. Dilution

TRUE OR FALSE: *(HINT)*

1. true	7. true	13. true	19. true
2. true	8. false	14. false	20. true
3. false	9. false	15. true	21. false
4. true	10. true	16. true	
5. false	11. true	17. false	
6. false	12. false	18. true	

MAKING CONNECTIONS: *(HINT)*

1. *Boats have motors that burn fossil fuels. The combustion of fossil fuels contributes to many different forms of air pollution. (Review chapter 19.) There are also problems with outboard motors that are unique: They allow the direct release of fuel into the water.*

2. *Just as aquatic and terrestrial ecosystems are connected, so are the problems of pollution in water and soil. Chemical spills that contaminate soils can seep into surface and groundwaters. Erosion of soil can cause water pollution. Soil can act as a reservoir for toxins that eventually make it into water.*

3. *The pumps allowed the villagers to access groundwater that is not contaminated with the pathogens that are prevalent in surface water.*

4. *Think about what happens when you start to boil a pot of water. Bubbles of air form. Warm water holds less oxygen. Water that has less oxygen supports a less diverse and, in most cases, less desirable community.*

MAKING DECISIONS: (HINT)

1. Review figure 21-12, which describes which pollutants are removed by each treatment. Tertiary treatment is necessary to remove phosphorus, nitrogen, heavy metals, and organic compounds. In the middle of an agricultural region, removal of phosphorus and nitrogen are particularly important to prevent adding these materials to local water supplies, which are already subjected to heavy agricultural runoff.

2. Chlorine is used to kill waterborne pathogens. Because the water in the United States is chlorinated, few Americans fear cholera, typhoid, or dysentery, diseases that can kill in a short time. However, recent evidence suggests that the chlorine used to decontaminate our water may be linked to other illnesses, such as cancer, that are not as immediate. There are few alternatives to chlorine. When Peru stopped chlorinating drinking water to prevent future cancers, thousands of people died of cholera. The dilemma is "Do we risk lives today or tomorrow?".

What do you think is the answer? What information would you try to gather in order to decide?

DOING SCIENCE: (HINT)

1. You will have to design a plan to monitor and sample the wells in the region. If there are no wells in the immediate vicinity, you may have to drill wells. Typically, under these conditions, wells are drilled in a circle around the contaminated well so that the direction of the flow of contamination can be determined.

11. Which of the following is NOT a classification of insecticides?

A. carbamates
B. chlorinated hydrocarbons

C. organophosphates
D. methyl bromides

12. Three mixes of herbicides were used during the Vietnam War. Only agent orange is associated with health problems in humans because

A. agent orange is a mixture of herbicides.
B. agent orange contains dioxin.
C. agent orange contains selective herbicides.
D. agent orange contains nonselective herbicides.

13. Organophosphates do not persist in the environment as long as chlorinated hydrocarbons because

A. they are more effective at killing pests
B. they are more easily degraded by microorganisms
C. they are not as effective at killing pests
D. they bioaccumulate

14. Raptors (birds of prey) typically have higher levels of fat-soluble toxins such as DDT than the prey they consume. The mice or fish have higher levels than the plants or plankton they consume. This is because:

A. fat-soluble molecules accumulate and concentrate as they move up the food chain
B. DDT enhances flavor so organisms choose to eat more of it
C. DDT is metabolized by mice and fish but not by birds
D. DDT causes thinning in the eggshells and reduces reproductive success in birds that have high levels in their tissues

15. If you are growing corn and you want to kill soybean plants that came up from seeds left in the soil from last year's crop, which of the following would be the best pesticide to choose?

A. broad-leaf herbicide
B. non-specific herbicide

C. grass herbicide
D. carbamates

FILL IN:

1. _____ are toxic chemicals that are used to kill pests, such as insects, weeds, fungi, nematodes, and rodents.

2. The _____ is attempting to help developing nations become more aware of dangerous pesticides.

3. Humans may be poisoned by exposure to large amounts of pesticides, whereas lower levels of many pesticides pose a long-term threat of _____.

4. _____, such as nicotine and pyrethrum, are easily degraded by microorganisms and, therefore, do not persist in the environment.

5. DDT is an example of a(n) _____ _____, an organic compound containing chlorine.

6. The _____, passed in 1938, recognized the need to regulate pesticides found in food but did not provide a means of regulation.

7. An updated FDCA, passed in 1958, contained an important section known as the _____ _____, which stated that no substance capable of causing cancer in test animals or in humans will be permitted in processed food.

8. _____ _____ involve the use of naturally occurring disease organisms, parasites, or predators to control pests.

9. Both inorganic compounds and botanicals are called _____ _____ _____ to distinguish them from the vast array of synthetic poisons in use today.

10. _____ are broad-spectrum insecticides derived from carbamic acid that are generally not as toxic to mammals as the organophosphates, although they still show broad non-target toxicity.

11. Chlorinated hydrocarbons such as DDT and aldrin are broad-spectrum _____.

12. The buildup of a pesticide in an organism's body is known as _____, or bioconcentration.

13. The cultivated field represents a very simple _____.

CHECKING WHAT YOU KNOW: (HINT)

MULTIPLE CHOICE: (HINT)

1. A	5. C	9. B	13. B
2. D	6. A	10. C	14. A
3. B	7. D	11. D	15. A
4. C	8. B	12. B	

FILL IN: (HINT)

1. Pesticide
2. Food and Agriculture Organization (FAO)
3. cancer
4. Botanicals
5. chlorinated hydrocarbon
6. Food, Drug, and Cosmetics Act (FDCA)
7. Delaney Clause
8. Biological controls
9. first-generation pesticides
10. Carbamates
11. insecticides
12. bioaccumulation
13. ecosystem
14. resistance management
15. sterile male technique
16. reproductive potential
17. Integrated pest management (IPM)
18. Synthetic botanicals
19. monoculture
20. narrow-spectrum pesticide
21. pests
22. entomologist
23. Bacillus thuringiensis (Bt)
24. Pheromones
25. DDT
26. pest
27. persistence
28. biological magnification
29. dioxins
30. endocrine disrupters
31. inert ingredients
32. Insecticides
33. Herbicides
34. Fungicides
35. Rodenticides
36. quarantine
37. scout-and-spray
38. Genetic engineering
39. genetic resistance
40. herbicides
41. Organophosphates
42. pesticide treadmill
43. calendar spraying

TRUE OR FALSE: (HINT)

1. false	5. true	9. false	13. true
2. true	6. false	10. false	14. false
3. false	7. true	11. true	
4. false	8. true	12. true	

PEOPLE WHO MATTER: (HINT)

1. Rachel Carson was a wildlife biologist who wrote the book "Silent Spring" that started the environmental movement. "Silent Spring" documented the environmental harm caused by the uncontrolled use of pesticides. There are several resources available for finding out more about Rachel Carson. The following two websites are good places to start.

http://www.rachelcarson.org/
http://www.cwru.edu/affil/wwwethics/carson/main.html

MAKING CONNECTIONS: (HINT)

1.

bird
bigger fish
small fish
phytoplankton

2. Pesticides sprayed on agricultural fields wash into streams , lakes, and rivers, and seep into groundwater. Both surface and groundwaters are the sources of drinking water.

MAKING DECISIONS: (HINT)

1. A catastrophic event, which releases large quantities of pesticide into the environment, would be an acute exposure that could have immediate toxic effects. The damage from this sort of exposure would be immediate and obvious. People could become sick and die very quickly. The low-level, long-term leakage would be a chronic exposure. The detrimental effects could appear many years later and only be seen as a slight increase in certain diseases, such as cancer.

DOING SCIENCE: (HINT)

1. DDT killed not only the target pest (in this case, an insect other than red scale) but many other insects, including the predators that held the population of red scale insects in check. With their predators absent (or present in greatly reduced numbers), the red scale insects experienced a population explosion.

CHAPTER 23 -- SOLID AND HAZARDOUS WASTES

LEARNING THE LANGUAGE:

biodegradable
biological magnification
bioremediation
bottom ash
compost
cullet
dematerialization
dioxins
electrostatic precipitator
environmental chemistry
environmental justice
fee-per-bag approach
fly ash
green chemistry
groundwater
hazardous waste
high-temperature incinerator
industrial ecosystem
integrated waste management
leachate
lime scrubber

mass burn incinerator
modular incinerators
mulch
municipal solid waste
nonmunicipal solid waste
open dumps
pesticide
petroleum
photodegradable
phytoremediation
polyvinyl chloride
principle of inherent safety
recycling
refuse-derived fuel incinerators
resource recovery facilities
reuse
sanitary landfill
source reduction
Superfund National Priorities List
surface water

CHECKING WHAT YOU KNOW:

MULTIPLE CHOICE:

1. Which of the following is NOT true of most of the citizens who attend meetings to discuss opening new landfill sites in their neighborhoods?

    A. They are looking for a way to dispose of solid waste properly.
    B. They are willing to try and reduce the amount of solid waste from their own homes.
    C. They are concerned about health and safety.
    D. They are willing to have the landfill located in their community.

2. The most comprehensive solution to the problem of solid waste is

    A. recycling
    B. reuse

    C. dematerialization
    D. integrated waste management

3. Which of the following is NOT a problem associated with incineration of solid waste?

A. ash production

B. air pollution

C. energy production

D. slag production

4. The Superfund National Priorities List

A. identifies sites that pose the greatest threat to human health and the environment.

B. identifies sites that have the greatest need for inclusion as wilderness areas.

C. identifies sites that have nuclear wastes.

D. identifies sites to build waste treatment and storage facilities.

5. What percentage of solid waste was composted in 1996?

A. 3.8
B. 16.7
C. 23.8
D. 55.7

6. What is the source of the hazardous waste nerve gas?

A. nuclear power plants

B. coolant in air conditioners

C. petroleum products

D. old military installations

7. What percentage of solid waste was sent to sanitary landfills in 1996?

A. 3.8
B. 16.7
C. 23.8
D. 55.7

8. Which of the following refers to a plan to prevent accidents by redesigning processes to use less hazardous chemicals:

A. the Superfund National Priorities List

B. the Environmental Protection Agency

C. environmental justice

D. the principle of inherent safety

9. Electrostatic precipitators produce _____.

   A. bottom ash   B. slag   C. fly ash   D. lime

10. The _____ plant has been shown to be effective in the phytoremediation of cesium-137.

   A. sunflower   C. cattail
   B. stonewort   D. Indian mustard

11. Manufacturing techniques that reduce the volume of waste and the amount of toxic substances in the waste are using a strategy called

   A. reuse   C. conservation
   B. source reduction   D. dematerialization

12. Which of the following types of pollutants are NOT cleaned up using phytoremediation?

   A. Lead from paint that peeled off a house and landed in the garden   C. Chlorofluorocarbons in the stratosphere over Antarctica

   B. Radioactive strontium in a field near the Chernobyl nuclear reactor   D. Trinitrotoluene that has leaked into the soil around a chemical dump

13. _____ are hazardous compounds found in electrical transformers and capacitors as well as older appliances.

   A. Dioxins   C. Chlorofluorocarbons (CFCs)
   B. Organic solvents   D. Polychlorinated biphenyls (PCBs)

14. Which of the following is a reuse of old tires?

   A. making rubberized asphalt   C. reef building on coastlines
   B. making garden hoses   D. making trash cans

15. Materials that will degrade only after being exposed to sunlight are called _____.

   A. biodegradable   C. photodegradable
   B. polymers   D. degradable

16. Which of the following is NOT commonly recycled?

    A. aluminum cans
    B. glass bottles
    C. newspapers
    D. ceramic dishes

17. Which of the following is NOT a source of hazardous waste?

    A. industrial processes
    B. mining
    C. organic gardening
    D. military activities

18. Which of the following is NOT true of open dumps?

    A. unsanitary
    B. methane production converted to energy
    C. infested with rats and flies
    D. no longer legally used for solid waste disposal

19. What is the greatest source of solid waste in the United States?

    A. agriculture   B. industry   C. mining   D. cities

20. Incinerators that will only burn the combustible fraction of solid waste are _____.

    A. refuse-derived fuel incinerators
    B. modular incinerators
    C. mass burn incinerators
    D. combustible incinerators

21. Which of the following will NOT reduce the amount of hazardous materials in solid waste?

    A. Find less hazardous materials to replace those currently used
    B. Use hazardous materials in less durable products
    C. Find ways to recycle products
    D. Buy fewer products that contain hazardous chemicals

22. _____ is the best way to reduce the risk of exposure to hazardous wastes.

    A. Source reduction
    B. Reuse
    C. Use of the plasma torch
    D. Recycling

23. Which of the following is NOT an appropriate mechanism to manage hazardous waste?

   A. source reduction
   B. dumping
   C. long-term storage
   D. conversion to less hazardous materials

24. A _____ breaks hazardous materials such as PCBs into nonhazardous gases.

   A. mass burn incinerator
   B. hanford nuclear reactor

   C. plasma torch
   D. modular incinerator

25. More than 40 percent of solid waste is

   A. metals
   B. yard wastes

   C. plastics
   D. paper

FILL IN:

1. According to the EPA, _____ scrap iron and steel produces 86 percent less air pollution and 76 percent less water pollution than mining and refining iron ore.

2. _____ involves collecting and reprocessing materials into new products.

3. _____ _____ _____ includes wastes from industry, agriculture, and mining and is produced in substantially larger amounts than municipal solid waste.

4. One way to detoxify hazardous organic compounds is by _____ _____ _____, which produces temperatures up to 10,000°C.

5. _____ is the use of bacteria and other microorganisms to break down hazardous waste.

6. Because _____ products break down only after being exposed to sunlight, they will not break down in a sanitary landfill.

7. _____ is the use of plants to absorb and accumulate toxic materials from the soil.

8. Industry and government agencies have stressed accident prevention through the _____, in which industrial processes are redesigned to involve less toxic materials so that dangerous accidents are prevented.

9. At _____ _____ _____, solid waste is either hand-sorted or separated using a variety of technologies, including magnets, screens, and conveyor belts.

10. Glass food and beverage containers are crushed to form _____ , which can be melted and used by glass manufacturers to make new products without any special adaptations in their factories.

11. Most _____ _____ _____ are designed to recover the energy produced from combustion.

12. Plastic is made from _____ that must be extracted from the ground and refined, producing both air and water pollution.

13. _____ is an increasingly important subdiscipline of chemistry in which commercially important chemical processes are redesigned to significantly reduce environmental harm.

14. In _____ _____ _____, a variety of options that minimize waste, including the 3 R's of waste prevention (reduce, reuse, and recycle), are incorporated into an overall waste management plan.

15. The _____ _____ movement is calling for special efforts to clean up hazardous sites in low-income neighborhoods, from inner-city streets to Indian reservations.

16. _____ _____ differ from open dumps in that the solid waste is placed in a hole, compacted, and covered with a thin layer of soil every day.

17. Many communities have reduced the volume of solid waste and encouraged reuse and recycling by charging households for each container of solid waste. This is the _____ _____ _____ approach.

18. If a sanitary landfill is operated in accordance with solid waste management-approved guidelines, it does not pollute local surface and _____ .

19. _____ _____ are towers in which a chemical spray neutralizes acidic gases.

20. _____ _____ give ash a positive electrical charge so that it adheres to negatively charged plates rather than going out the chimney.

21. _____ and much can be used in public parks and playgrounds, for landscaping, or as part of the daily soil cover at sanitary landfills; or they can be sold to gardeners.

22. Newer landfills possess a double liner system and use sophisticated systems to collect _____, the liquid that seeps through the solid waste.

23. The progressive decrease in the size and weight of a product as a result of technological improvements is called _____.

24. _____ _____ _____ consists of solid materials discarded by homes, office buildings, retail stores, restaurants, schools, hospitals, prisons, libraries, and other commercial and institutional facilities.

25. _____ _____, which accounts for about one percent of the solid waste stream in the United States, includes chemicals that are dangerously reactive, corrosive, explosive, or toxic.

26. _____, compounds formed as unwanted by-products during the combustion of chlorine compounds, are known to cause several kinds of cancer in laboratory animals, but the data are conflicting on their carcinogenicity in humans.

27. _____ _____, a common component of many plastics, may release dioxin and other toxic compounds when incinerated.

28. _____ _____ also known as slag, is the residual ash left at the bottom of the incinerator when combustion is completed.

29. One example of _____ is refillable glass beverage bottles.

30. _____ plastics are decomposed by microorganisms such as bacteria.

31. DDT, dioxins, and PCBs accumulate in fatty tissues and are subject to _____ _____ in food webs.

32. Unlike bottom ash, _____ _____ usually contains more toxic materials, including heavy metals and possibly dioxins.

33. The old sites of solid waste disposal, _____ _____, were unsanitary, malodorous places in which disease-carrying vermin such as rats and flies proliferated.

34. In _____ only the combustible portion of solid waste is burned.

35. _____ _____ are solids, liquids, and gases that pose a real or potential threat to the environment or to human health.

36. _____ _____ are small and burn all solid wastes; they are built in factories.

37. The strategy of designing and manufacturing products to reduce the volume of solid waste and the amount of hazardous materials in them is called _____ _____.

38. Toxic or hazardous waste sites that end up on the _____ will get federal funds to support cleanup.

TRUE OR FALSE:

1. True   False   Bioremediation is faster than traditional hazardous waste disposal methods.

2. True   False   Tires produce as much heat as coal and often generate less pollution.

3. True   False   Most people are happy to have solid waste disposal facilities in their communities.

4. True   False   Sanitary landfills are more likely to harbor disease-carrying vermin than open dumps.

5. True   False   Consumers can reduce waste by decreasing their consumption of products.

6. True   False   Reuse saves energy and reduces pollution significantly as compared to recycling.

7. True   False   Composting is a great way to dispose of yard waste without filling up valuable landfill space.

8. True   False   One of the most urgent problems of industrialized nations is the disposal of solid and hazardous wastes, which increase in quantity each year.

9. True   False   Recycling is the best way to reduce hazardous waste.

PEOPLE WHO MATTER:

1. Who is Jack Richard Simplot, and what has he done to help protect the environment? Can you think of other examples where similar techniques could be used?

MAKING CONNECTIONS:

1. Dioxins are emitted in smoke. They end up falling on bodies of water, the soil, and the surfaces of plants. How do they get into the food web from these locations?

2. Pick a product such as aluminum cans that you commonly recycle. Draw a "biogeochemical cycle" for this product. Consider the biological portion of the cycle (comparable to when the element would be part of a living organism) to be when the material is in your possession.

MAKING DECISIONS:

1. "Paper or plastic?" Chances are if you go to the grocery store today, you will be asked some version of this question. What factors should you consider before you answer this question?

2. The worst environmental degradation is often located closest to poor neighborhoods. These people are often unable to afford health care, so the effects of this proximity to environmental hazards is exacerbated. List some reasons this situation might exist. What can be done to prevent this from happening in the future?

DOING SCIENCE:

1. Biological degradation of PCBs in deep soils and groundwater is not feasible today. How would you begin to look for ways to make this degradation more likely?

CHECKING WHAT YOU KNOW: (HINT)

MULTIPLE CHOICE: (HINT)

1. D	8. D	15. C	22. A
2. D	9. C	16. D	23. B
3. C	10. A	17. C	24. C
4. A	11. B	18. B	25. D
5. A	12. C	19. C	
6. D	13. D	20. A	
7. D	14. C	21. B	

FILL IN: (HINT)

1. recycling
2. Recycling
3. Nonmunicipal solid waste
4. high-temperature incineration
5. Bioremediation
6. photodegradable
7. Phytoremediation
8. principle of inherent safety
9. resource recovery facilities
10. cullet
11. mass burn incinerators
12. petroleum
13. Environmental chemistry or Green chemistry
14. integrated waste management
15. environmental justice
16. Sanitary landfills
17. fee-per-bag approach
18. groundwater
19. Lime scrubbers
20. Electrostatic precipitators
21. Compost
22. leachate
23. dematerialization
24. Municipal solid waste
25. Hazardous waste
26. Dioxins
27. Polyvinyl chloride
28. Bottom ash
29. reuse
30. Biodegradable
31. biological magnification
32. fly ash
33. open dumps
34. refuse-derived fuel incinerators
35. Hazardous wastes
36. Modular incinerators
37. source reduction
38. Superfund National Priorities List

TRUE OR FALSE: (HINT)

1. false	4. false	7. true
2. true	5. true	8. true
3. false	6. true	9. false

PEOPLE WHO MATTER: (HINT)

1. Read Envirobrief "An Industrial Ecosystem" on page 543. Think of other examples that could make maximum use of waste products.

MAKING CONNECTIONS: (HINT)

1. Materials that land on the soil and water can be incorporated into plant or algal tissues. They can also be absorbed into other organisms. Dioxin that enters plant tissue or that is consumed along with the plant material it is coating becomes part of the body of the primary consumers. Primary consumers are eaten by secondary consumers. Secondary consumers are eaten by tertiary consumers and so on. Since dioxin accumulates in the fatty tissues and is not removed from the body, it is concentrated as it moves up the food web, a process called biological magnification.

2.

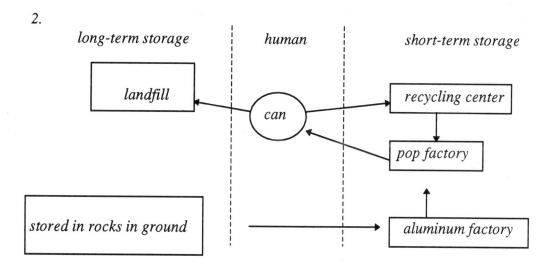

MAKING DECISIONS: (HINT)

1.

Paper	Plastic
made from trees	*made from petroleum products*
could be recycled	*could be recycled*
loss of trees --> increased CO_2 --> global warming (unless logged forests are replanted)	*environmental impact of mining/refining oil*
biodegradable	*not biodegradable*
renewable resources	*nonrenewable resources*
bulky to carry	*easy to carry*
etc...	*etc...*

Gather all the facts you can and then make the decision that is right for who you are, where you are, and what you are doing. Do your best to minimize the environmental impact of your choice. If you must choose something that causes more harm than you like in one area of your life, try to compensate in another area.

2. Reasons for current situations...
- *Poor have no money for lawyers and protests?*
- *Land values are low in poor neighborhoods, so it is economical to locate such waste facilities there?*
- *Land values are low near such facilities, so it is more economical for the poor to live there?*
- *Racism?*

Probably the best way to insure that the poor are not unnecessarily exposed to toxic wastes is to reduce the amounts of toxic wastes produced. Laws could be established to protect poor neighborhoods from future environmental problems --zoning, compensation, costs for moving, access to medicine...

DOING SCIENCE: (HINT)

1. Create laboratory conditions that mimic situations where PCBs are in groundwater or deep in soils. Set up experiments to see what needs to be added to these environments to promote the growth of bacteria that carryout biological degradation of PCBs. Perhaps the problem is lack of nutrients, improper temperature, too little or too much water, or lack of oxygen. Perhaps it is simply a matter of getting the bacteria into these areas.

Another approach would be to identify bacteria that live in these environments and see if any of them can degrade PCBs. If not, you could try to genetically engineer bacteria that can live in these environments and degrade PCBs.

CHAPTER 24 -- TOMORROW'S WORLD

Now that you have finished your current study of the environment, it is time to take a few minutes to reflect about what you have learned. The following series of questions do not have answers. You must use the information you have learned and the resources you have learned to access to figure out the best answer you can. These questions can be the basis of some interesting discussions with your friends and family. Use them to spark thought, conversation, and hopefully concern about our environment and the problems facing it.

1. Pick an organism that you fear or dislike, for example snakes or spiders. Learn all that you can about that organism. Now imagine what would happen to the natural ecosystem if this organism was completely removed from the environment. What would be the effect on the flow of energy? How will other predators and prey be affected? Will humans benefit, be harmed, or largely be unaffected by the removal of this species?

2. Keep track of everything you consume for an entire day. Include not only the obvious items such as food and other products, but also energy. Try to figure out the real environmental cost of what you consume. Justify your consumption. Craft a plan to reduce your consumption.

3. If you are using this book as a student, you are probably planning to make a move after you graduate to start a new job. Imagine that you can choose a job in a remote area where you will be able to live in a house in the woods or an urban job in a large city. What are all the environmental implications of each of these possibilities? What are the personal choices you must make?

4. What can you do to reduce the risk of exposure to pesticides and harmful chemicals in your everyday life? Think not only about choices you make to directly affect your exposure, but also think about indirect choices that affect the amount of toxins introduced into the environment.

5. What choices can you make in your daily life that affect biodiversity? Think about what you consume, where you live, and how you act.

6. Imagine that you are going to be one of the first humans to colonize Mars. What do you need to survive in this environment?

7. What is the relationship between human population and environmental harm? What do you think about population control? Is it necessary? Who should determine who has children and how many they have? What ways currently exist to control population?

8. What do you perceive to be the biggest environmental threat? Why do you think this is the biggest problem? What data do you have to support your view? What personal concerns, religious beliefs, and political positions affect your decision?

9. Who do you think is most responsible for the state of the environment? People in industrial nations? Developing nations? Ancestors?

10. Many science fiction writers write about time travel and the potential implications associated with stepping on a butterfly while visiting the dinosaurs. How does this concept relate to what you have learned in this text?